LIVING LITURGY™

FOR EXTRAORDINARY MINISTERS OF HOLY COMMUNION

Year A • 2014

Joyce Ann Zimmerman, C.PP.S.
Kathleen Harmon, S.N.D. de N.
Christopher W. Conlon, S.M.

LITURGICAL PRESS
Collegeville, Minnesota

www.litpress.org

Design by Ann Blattner. Art by Martin Erspamer, OSB

ISSN 1933-3129

ISBN 978-0-8146-3502-5

Presented to

---

*in grateful appreciation
for ministering as an
Extraordinary Minister
of
Holy Communion*

(date)

USING THIS RESOURCE

Extraordinary ministers of Holy Communion are called to serve the Christian community by ministering the Body and Blood of Christ to the Body of Christ, for by baptism we are all made members of the Body of Christ. Rather than a "status symbol" in the liturgical community, these ministers are servants of the servants, as Jesus himself showed us at the Last Supper. They are called "extraordinary" not because of any personal worthiness or honor but because the "ordinary" ministers of Holy Communion are bishops, priests, deacons, or instituted acolytes. In the typical parish situation, however, large numbers of the faithful come forward for Communion, and so in most cases lay members of the parish are designated as "extraordinary" ministers so that the Communion procession does not become disproportionately long.

Preparing for this ministry

As with all ministry, extraordinary ministers of Holy Communion must prepare themselves in order to serve their sisters and brothers in Christ well. This book is intended to be a guide and resource for that preparation. Each Sunday and some key festival days are laid out with prayer and reflections to help the Communion minister prepare each week, even when he or she is not scheduled for ministry. Some of the language of the text implies a group is present for the preparation; these texts are conveniently worded for when two or more extraordinary ministers gather for preparation, or for when these texts are shared in the context of the rite of Holy Communion with the homebound and sick.

Holy Communion for the homebound and sick

Jesus' preaching of the Good News in the Gospel is made visible by his many and varied good works on behalf of others. Perhaps more than any other group, Jesus reaches out with his healing touch to those who are sick, and this compassionate ministry continues today in the life of the church. One of the many blessings of parishes who have extraordinary ministers of Holy Communion is that those who are sick or homebound within parishes or those in hospitals and other care centers can share in the liturgical life of the parish more frequently. These ministers are reminded that the sick and suffering share in a special way in Jesus' passion. The ministers can bring hope and consolation and the strength of the Bread of Life to those who seem cut off from active participation in parish life.

Adapting this resource for Holy Communion for the homebound and sick

It is presumed that each Communion minister is familiar with the rites for Communion of the sick. There is a brief rite for those in hospitals or other care centers; this shorter rite is used when the circumstances would not permit the longer rite. The longer rite is used in ordinary circumstances and includes a Liturgy of the Word preceding the Communion rite. When using the longer rite, the opening and closing prayer given for each Sunday or festival included in this book would nicely round out the beginning and end of the service; the gospel is conveniently included to proclaim the word, and a reflection (also included for each Sunday or festival) might be shared.

Privilege and dignity

It is indeed a unique blessing to serve members of the parish as extraordinary ministers of Holy Communion, both at the parish Mass and by bringing Communion to the sick and homebound. The parish's presence through ministry to the sick and homebound is a particular sign of their dignity as members of the Body of Christ. The Communion minister is in a unique position to bring hope and comfort to those who may find little in life to comfort them. May this ministry always be a sign of Jesus' great love and compassion for all his Father's beloved children!

Jesus calls us to "stay awake" and prepare for the coming judgment. As we begin our prayer and reflection, let us open our hearts to hear God's word and encounter God's Presence . . .

Prayer

O God who is ever present to us, come to us even now as we prepare to celebrate the incarnation of your divine Son. As we look to his coming in glory, may we do all we can now in our own lives to prepare well for the final judgment that is to come. We ask this through Christ our Lord. **Amen**.

Gospel (Matt 24:37-44)

Jesus said to his disciples: "As it was in the days of Noah, so it will be at the coming of the Son of Man. In those days before the flood, they were eating and drinking, marrying and giving in marriage, up to the day that Noah entered the ark. They did not know until the flood came and carried them all away. So will it be also at the coming of the Son of Man. Two men will be out in the field; one will be taken, and one will be left. Two women will be grinding at the mill; one will be taken, and one will be left. Therefore, stay awake! For you do not know on which day your Lord will come. Be sure of this: if the master of the house had known the hour of night when the thief was coming, he would have stayed awake and not let his house be broken into. So too, you also must be prepared, for at an hour you do not expect, the Son of Man will come."

Brief Silence

For Reflection

Jesus admonishes us to "stay awake." While he is directly speaking to the future event of the coming of the Son of Man (actually, he himself in all his glory) at the end of time, we can also understand staying awake as related to present events. Our wakefulness and readiness *now* prepare us for his future coming. "As it was in the days . . . so it will be"—with these words Jesus points to patterns in human conduct. Humans have been both unfaithful and faithful to God's ways; have not paid attention, have paid attention to God's instructions; have not been awake, have stayed awake to God's comings. The people in the days of Noah did not know that the flood was coming; Jesus' hearers did not know when the Son of Man would come. We, however, do know that Jesus has come, has taught us the way of faithfulness, has brought us salvation. We need only to "stay awake." Advent is about *our* coming to God. Our staying awake is a matter of preparing well for the divine Guest who dwells in our hearts now and always.

✦ Those receiving Holy Communion from me are processing to the mountain of God, and I see . . .

Brief Silence

Prayer

Ever-present God, you come to us in Holy Communion, through other people, in the many acts of goodness and kindness we see every day. Open us to your many ways of coming to us, that we may prepare well for your final coming. We ask this through Christ our Lord. **Amen**.

John the Baptist prepared for the coming of Christ by calling the people to a baptism of repentance. Let us prepare for our prayer by opening our hearts to the Presence of the Spirit in whom we were baptized . . .

Prayer

O God, you come to us in the desert of our difficult times and in the fullness of our joyful times. May the Holy Spirit we have received at our baptism always shine forth in all we do. May we be on fire to spread the Good News of reconciliation and forgiveness. We ask this through Christ our Lord. **Amen**.

Gospel (Matt 3:1-12)

John the Baptist appeared, preaching in the desert of Judea and saying, "Repent, for the kingdom of heaven is at hand!" It was of him that the prophet Isaiah had spoken when he said: / *A voice of one crying out in the desert, / Prepare the way of the Lord, / make straight his paths.* / John wore clothing made of camel's hair and had a leather belt around his waist. His food was locusts and wild honey. At that time Jerusalem, all Judea, and the whole region around the Jordan were going out to him and were being baptized by him in the Jordan River as they acknowledged their sins.

When he saw many of the Pharisees and Sadducees coming to his baptism, he said to them, "You brood of vipers! Who warned you to flee from the coming wrath? Produce good fruit as evidence of your repentance. And do not presume to say to yourselves, 'We have Abraham as our father.' For I tell you, God can raise up children to Abraham from these stones. Even now the ax lies at the root of the trees. Therefore every tree that does not bear good fruit will be cut down and thrown into the fire. I am baptizing you with water, for repentance, but the one who is coming after me is mightier than I. I am not worthy to carry his sandals. He will baptize you with the Holy Spirit and fire. His winnowing fan is in his hand. He will clear his threshing floor and gather his wheat into his barn, but the chaff he will burn with unquenchable fire."

Brief Silence

For Reflection

John the Baptist prepared "the way of the LORD" by calling the people to repentance so they would not be "thrown into the fire" of "the coming wrath." John announced impending judgment and offered a baptism of repentance. John also announced One to come who would enact that judgment and bring a baptism in the Holy Spirit and fire. The fire of judgment will destroy those who are fruitless; the fire of the Spirit will help the faithful bear good fruit. Advent is, in the end, about jumping into the fire. This is our time to embrace our baptism, to allow the Holy Spirit to set us afire anew for living the Gospel. The image of fire reminds us that we are purified and made holy by our baptism; we receive the Holy Spirit and God's Life is within us. This is what empowers us to bear fruit. All we need to do is say yes to God's will and be faithful to our baptismal call. We also remember that baptism plunges us into the mystery of Christ's dying and rising. Conforming ourselves to Christ, we take on our own challenges to die to self for the sake of others.

✦ The "good fruit" which the Eucharist is nourishing in me this Advent is . . . I am set afire to share this good fruit with others when . . .

Brief Silence

Prayer

God of light and fire, you send your Holy Spirit to stir us to good works done in your Son's name. May we be afire with your love, bringing goodness and compassion to all those we meet. We ask this through Christ our Lord. **Amen.**

THE IMMACULATE CONCEPTION OF THE BLESSED VIRGIN MARY

On this solemnity of the Immaculate Conception we look to Mary's holiness of life as a model for our own living. Let us reflect on how faithful we have been to our baptismal call to holiness . . .

Prayer

God of holiness, you made Mary pure and holy from the very moment of her conception. Help us to turn to her in times of temptation and distress, learn from her fidelity, and be open to the gift of grace you give us. We ask this through Christ our Lord. **Amen**.

Gospel (Luke 1:26-38)

The angel Gabriel was sent from God to a town of Galilee called Nazareth, to a virgin betrothed to a man named Joseph, of the house of David, and the virgin's name was Mary. And coming to her, he said, "Hail, full of grace! The Lord is with you." But she was greatly troubled at what was said and pondered what sort of greeting this might be. Then the angel said to her, "Do not be afraid, Mary, for you have found favor with God. Behold, you will conceive in your womb and bear a son, and you shall name him Jesus. He will be great and will be called Son of the Most High, and the Lord God will give him the throne of David his father, and he will rule over the house of Jacob forever, and of his Kingdom there will be no end." But Mary said to the angel, "How can this be, since I have no relations with a man?" And the angel said to her in reply, "The Holy Spirit will come upon you, and the power of the Most High will overshadow you. Therefore the child to be born will be called holy, the Son of God. And behold, Elizabeth, your relative, has also conceived a son in her old age, and this is the sixth month for her who was called barren; for nothing will be impossible for God." Mary said, "Behold, I am the handmaid of

10

the Lord. May it be done to me according to your word." Then the angel departed from her.

Brief Silence

For Reflection

In this annunciation account, Mary is twice troubled: first, when the angel Gabriel greets her as one "full of grace" and, second, when she is told she will conceive in spite of having had "no relations with a man." Yes, Mary was troubled—she struggled, just like us. She questioned, just like us. She wondered, just like us. At the same time that Mary was twice troubled, this gospel also discloses a double gift: first, God's gracious gift to Mary of holiness and the call to bear the incarnate One; second, Mary's gracious gift to us of her yes response, "May it be done to me." The same gift of God's holiness is offered to us, calling forth our own gift of "May it be done to me." Holiness is God's favor bestowed on us, God's divine Life dwelling within us which establishes a unique relationship with God and each other. And just as Mary gave the gift of the divine Son to all of us, so are we to give the gift of that same Son who dwells within us to others. These gifts call forth a "May it be done to me" from each of us. Our yes is our gift to each other.

✦ Being given the gift of holiness means to me . . .

Brief Silence

Prayer

O holy God, your divine Life dwells within us through the power of the Holy Spirit. May we always say yes to your holy will, be faithful to the gifts you have given us, and share generously with others these gifts. We ask this through Christ our Lord. **Amen**.

Jesus reveals himself as the One who is to come, the promised Savior. As we prepare to pray and reflect, let us open ourselves to encounter this Jesus who saves . . .

Prayer

O God, you sent your divine Son so we could hear and see the marvels of your goodness. Be with us as we prepare to celebrate the incarnation of Jesus and help us to see him and his good works in the people and events around us. We ask this through Christ our Lord. **Amen**.

Gospel (Matt 11:2-11)

When John the Baptist heard in prison of the works of the Christ, he sent his disciples to Jesus with this question, "Are you the one who is to come, or should we look for another?" Jesus said to them in reply, "Go and tell John what you hear and see: the blind regain their sight, the lame walk, lepers are cleansed, the deaf hear, the dead are raised, and the poor have the good news proclaimed to them. And blessed is the one who takes no offense at me."

As they were going off, Jesus began to speak to the crowds about John, "What did you go out to the desert to see? A reed swayed by the wind? Then what did you go out to see? Someone dressed in fine clothing? Those who wear fine clothing are in royal palaces. Then why did you go out? To see a prophet? Yes, I tell you, and more than a prophet. This is the one about whom it is written: / *Behold, I am sending my messenger ahead of you; / he will prepare your way before you.* / Amen, I say to you, among those born of women there has been none greater than John the Baptist; yet the least in the kingdom of heaven is greater than he."

Brief Silence

For Reflection

What makes John great is that he recognizes in "the works of the Christ" the person and presence of the Messiah—"the one who is to come." This is exactly our Advent challenge: to see in the goodness around us the works of Jesus and the Presence of "the Christ." Advent calls us to look deeper and then to trust what we see. Whom we discover depends upon what we see. When people went to the desert, they saw and heard exactly what they expected to see and hear: a prophet dressed in animal skins calling them to repentance. When they looked at Jesus, however, they did not see and hear what they were expecting from the Messiah. The gospel challenge is to open ourselves to seeing something—Someone— different from our expectations. John's question must become our own: Is Jesus the One for us, or are we really looking for another? In trying to answer the question of Jesus' identity, we cannot rely only on the authority of others found in creeds or catechisms. Our answer must also come from our own personal experience of Jesus and the good fruit of his life and ministry.

✦ I see "the Christ" in the face of the communicants I serve when I . . .

Brief Silence

Prayer

God of surprises, you send the Presence of your divine Son to us, teaching us to see his Presence and hear his voice teaching us the Good News of salvation. Help us to live as he taught us and to serve him faithfully as did John the Baptist all the days of our lives. We ask this through Christ our Lord. **Amen**.

Joseph believed and obeyed the God who spoke to him in a dream. Let us open our hearts to God's speaking to us during our prayer and reflect on how God is made present to us in our daily living . . .

Prayer

God of power and might, your Spirit overshadowed Mary and she conceived the divine Son in her virgin womb. Be with us as we strive, like St. Joseph, to discern your path for us and to do whatever you ask of us. We ask this through Christ our Lord. **Amen**.

Gospel (Matt 1:18-24)

This is how the birth of Jesus Christ came about. When his mother Mary was betrothed to Joseph, but before they lived together, she was found with child through the Holy Spirit. Joseph her husband, since he was a righteous man, yet unwilling to expose her to shame, decided to divorce her quietly. Such was his intention when, behold, the angel of the Lord appeared to him in a dream and said, "Joseph, son of David, do not be afraid to take Mary your wife into your home. For it is through the Holy Spirit that this child has been conceived in her. She will bear a son and you are to name him Jesus, because he will save his people from their sins." All this took place to fulfill what the Lord had said through the prophet: / *Behold, the virgin shall conceive and bear a son, / and they shall name him Emmanuel, /* which means "God is with us." When Joseph awoke, he did as the angel of the Lord had commanded him and took his wife into his home.

Brief Silence

For Reflection

In this gospel, the state of affairs is not what it appears to be. Mary is not unfaithful, but faithful. Mary is with child, but a virgin. The infant is not only an earthly child, but also a heavenly One. Yet the infant is not heaven-bound, but an earthbound Emmanuel. Joseph is not the father, but in a father's role names the Child Jesus. When the Spirit of God is at work, and we cooperate as did Mary and Joseph, something altogether new happens: mystery abounds, "God is with us." Mystery curbs our judgments and opens us to the workings of the Holy Spirit all around us. Twice the gospel emphasizes that these events happened "through the Holy Spirit." The incarnation and redemption are wholly God's work, not our own. We are called to cooperate with God's plan. If we judge too quickly, especially based on merely what appears to be, we may easily miss God's call to participate in such great events. If God chose such people as Joseph and Mary to cooperate in the divine plan of salvation, is it not reasonable to think that the Son's continued Presence in the world is brought about by us?

✦ My daily life witnesses to "God is with us" whenever I . . .

Brief Silence

Prayer

God of Spirit and truth, you are present to us and call us to be attentive to that divine Presence in our everyday lives. Help us to feel the touch of your choosing us to be your beloved children, strengthen us to bring your Presence to others, and be with us as we open ourselves to the saving grace you so freely offer us. We ask this through Christ our Lord. **Amen**.

Christmas celebrates a great mystery: the Light of the world comes to us. Let us open our hearts to the Presence of this Light in our midst as we begin our prayer . . .

Prayer

Saving God, your divine Son was present at the first utterance of your creative word. May that Word continue to re-create in us divine Light and Love so that we might celebrate the Christmas mystery with joy and peace. We ask this through Christ our Lord. **Amen**.

Gospel (John 1:1-18; At the Mass during the Day)

In the beginning was the Word, / and the Word was with God, / and the Word was God. / He was in the beginning with God. / All things came to be through him, / and without him nothing came to be. / What came to be through him was life, / and this life was the light of the human race; / the light shines in the darkness, / and the darkness has not overcome it.

A man named John was sent from God. He came for testimony, to testify to the light, so that all might believe through him. He was not the light, but came to testify to the light. The true light, which enlightens everyone, was coming into the world. / He was in the world, / and the world came to be through him, / but the world did not know him. / He came to what was his own, / but his own people did not accept him.

But to those who did accept him he gave power to become children of God, to those who believe in his name, who were born not by natural generation nor by human choice nor by a man's decision but of God. / And the Word became flesh / and made his dwelling among us, / and we saw his glory, / the glory as of the Father's only Son, / full of grace and truth.

John testified to him and cried out, saying, "This was he of whom I said, 'The one who is coming after me ranks ahead of me because he existed before me.'" From his fullness we have all received, grace in place of grace, because while the law was given through Moses, grace and truth came through Jesus Christ. No one has ever seen God. The only Son, God, who is at the Father's side, has revealed him.

Brief Silence

For Reflection

In the beginning, the book of Genesis tells us, our world was a formless void and darkness covered it (Gen 1:1-2). All it took to burst this darkness was God's word: "Let there be lights" (Gen 1:14ff.) and they were. Such a powerful word God spoke at the beginning of creation. God speaks, and creation happens. In time, Jesus is revealed as the eternal Word of God who, by his birth, "made his dwelling among us." This is an even more powerful Word than that spoken at the beginning of creation. Jesus, in himself, reveals the unseen God to all humanity. God is present to us in a new, incarnated way, one like us in all things except sin. What is asked of us in response to this Gift-revelation is surprising: we need only to accept Christ through whom we share in light, glory, grace, and truth—gifts given to us from God's fullness. The Christmas mystery is not only about Jesus' birth, but also about our own birth into the very Life of God. It would seem like such a small thing—to accept Christ—to receive so much in return: fullness of Life in God.

✦ I see the Light of the world in others when . . . They see that Light in me when . . .

Brief Silence

Prayer

God of light and darkness, you sent your Son to be our Light leading us to fullness of Life in you. Open us to the many ways Jesus is present to us and help us to be his faithful Presence to all we meet. We ask this through Christ our Lord. **Amen**.

The readings for this feast remind us that holiness for families is not dependent upon perfection or easy roads. As Mary and Joseph show us, holiness is dependent upon faithful obedience to God. Let us reflect on how faithful we have been to doing God's will . . .

Prayer

Holy God, we praise your name for the majesty of your goodness. Help us to overcome whatever obstacles stand in the way of growing in the Life you have given us, calling us to be your holy people. We ask this through Christ our Lord. **Amen**.

Gospel (Matt 2:13-15, 19-23)

When the magi had departed, behold, the angel of the Lord appeared to Joseph in a dream and said, "Rise, take the child and his mother, flee to Egypt, and stay there until I tell you. Herod is going to search for the child to destroy him." Joseph rose and took the child and his mother by night and departed for Egypt. He stayed there until the death of Herod, that what the Lord had said through the prophet might be fulfilled, *Out of Egypt I called my son.*

When Herod had died, behold, the angel of the Lord appeared in a dream to Joseph in Egypt and said, "Rise, take the child and his mother and go to the land of Israel, for those who sought the child's life are dead." He rose, took the child and his mother, and went to the land of Israel. But when he heard that Archelaus was ruling over Judea in place of his father Herod, he was afraid to go back there. And because he had been warned in a dream, he departed for the region of Galilee. He went and dwelt in a town called Nazareth, so that what had been spoken through the prophets might be fulfilled, *He shall be called a Nazorean.*

Brief Silence

For Reflection

To Joseph is given the revelation that danger is at hand and the Holy Family must flee to Egypt. To him is given the further revelation that it is safe to return to their homeland. Whether going or coming, Joseph is attentive to both the needs of his family and the overtures of God's Presence and guidance. He is head of the Holy Family: one in which the members discern God's will, risk change for each other's growth and good, and are united in fidelity to God and each other. The Holy Family is not exempt from life-threatening difficulties. Rather, it is in the midst of difficulty that their holiness is tested, deepened, and revealed as a faithful and obedient response to God. This feast calls us to be this same kind of holy family. All the wonderful gifts of grace bestowed upon the Holy Family—Jesus' miraculous conception by the Holy Spirit, Joseph's being reassured in taking the pregnant Mary into his home, the virgin birth, adoration of the infant by angels and shepherds and magi—did not preserve this family from hardship. Yet they responded faithfully and obediently to God's messages and will for them. They trusted God's ways.

✦ I relate to those with whom I may live, work, and minister in these holy ways . . .

Brief Silence

Prayer

O God, you protect and care for those whom you call to holiness. May we hear that divine call, respond in obedience to your holy will, and grow in our love and adoration of you. We ask this through Christ our Lord. **Amen**.

During our reflection and prayer honoring Mary, the Mother of God, may we draw closer to the Son she bore and ask for his mercy . . .

Prayer

O God, you revealed the birth of your divine Son to shepherds who hastened to find him and adore him. Help us to open ourselves to his saving Presence and, like the shepherds, to make known to others the Good News of your offer of salvation. We ask this through Christ our Lord. **Amen**.

Gospel (Luke 2:16-21)

The shepherds went in haste to Bethlehem and found Mary and Joseph, and the infant lying in the manger. When they saw this, they made known the message that had been told them about this child. All who heard it were amazed by what had been told them by the shepherds. And Mary kept all these things, reflecting on them in her heart. Then the shepherds returned, glorifying and praising God for all they had heard and seen, just as it had been told to them.

When eight days were completed for his circumcision, he was named Jesus, the name given him by the angel before he was conceived in the womb.

Brief Silence

For Reflection

Mary models for us a way of faithful living. She was present to her infant Son, pondered God's will and ways, was obedient to all God asked of her. She opened her entire being to God, contemplating the Word in her heart and bearing the Word in her body. We most fully imitate what our mother Mary modeled for us when we ourselves contemplate God's Word in our hearts and embody that Word in our daily living. What characterizes Mary, then, and all of us who call her mother is openness to God's Presence, contemplation of that divine Presence and what it means for our daily living, and obedience to God's will for us. With Mary we "keep these things, reflecting on them in [our] heart[s]"; like Mary, we assume a contemplative stance toward God's marvelous deeds of salvation, recognizing that they are a mystery to be lived. God revealed the divine will to Mary for her part in the plan of salvation; she responded with a yes which she contemplated throughout her life. Christmas reveals to us God's will for our salvation and asks of us our contemplative yes response.

✦ I imitate Mary's prayerful reflectiveness when I . . . This bears fruit in my daily living in these ways . . .

Brief Silence

Prayer

God of salvation, you gave us Mary as our mother to show us the way to contemplate in our hearts the great mystery of salvation. Through her intercession may we grow in our eagerness to say yes to whatever you ask of us by contemplating your ways in our hearts. We ask this through Christ our Lord. **Amen**.

During the time of Epiphany we celebrate Jesus who is the "newborn king" come to reveal himself to all people. Let us open our hearts to seek him during our reflection and prayer . . .

Prayer

Loving God, you created the great lights in the heavens to guide us through the darkness of life. May we be as diligent as the magi in coming to your Presence, open the treasures of our hearts to praise you, and bow before you in humble adoration. We ask this through Christ our Lord. **Amen**.

Gospel (Matt 2:1-12)

When Jesus was born in Bethlehem of Judea, in the days of King Herod, behold, magi from the east arrived in Jerusalem, saying, "Where is the newborn king of the Jews? We saw his star at its rising and have come to do him homage." When King Herod heard this, he was greatly troubled, and all Jerusalem with him. Assembling all the chief priests and the scribes of the people, he inquired of them where the Christ was to be born. They said to him, "In Bethlehem of Judea, for thus it has been written through the prophet: / *And you, Bethlehem, land of Judah, / are by no means least among the rulers of Judah; / since from you shall come a ruler, / who is to shepherd my people Israel." /* Then Herod called the magi secretly and ascertained from them the time of the star's appearance. He sent them to Bethlehem and said, "Go and search diligently for the child. When you have found him, bring me word, that I too may go and do him homage." After their audience with the king they set out. And behold, the star that they had seen at its rising preceded them, until it came and stopped over the place where the child was. They were overjoyed at seeing the star, and on entering the house they saw the child with Mary his mother. They prostrated themselves and did him homage. Then they opened their treasures and offered him gifts of gold, frankincense, and myrrh. And having been warned in a dream not to return to Herod, they departed for their country by another way.

Brief Silence

For Reflection

Arriving at Jerusalem, the magi thought they had come to the birthplace of "the newborn king of the Jews," for Jerusalem was the traditional home of the Jewish king. Of course this is where this king would be—in the city of kings. But the "newborn king" was not where they expected to find him. He was in Bethlehem, the home of David before he was made king, when he was still a simple shepherd boy. This king "who is to shepherd . . . Israel" was not born in a palace, but in a simple abode; was not given homage by Jewish elite, but by foreigners; was not given only gifts acknowledging his kingship, but also a gift of myrrh pointing to his passion; was not to be limited in his reign to the Jewish nation, but would reign over all peoples. In Christ, God's light of salvation shines forth (is manifested) for all people. Magi followed the light and found the Savior of the world. The magi came to Bethlehem and found the Light. Where do *we* expect to find this Light, this "newborn king," and who do *we* expect him to be?

✦ When I expect to see the face of the "newborn king" in the faces of those coming to receive Holy Communion, what happens is . . .

Brief Silence

Prayer

O God who fulfills all expectation, be with us as we follow the Light of your divine Son. Strengthen us to be faithful followers who will one day share in the fullness of Light and Life with him. We ask this through Christ our Lord. **Amen.**

At Jesus' baptism his identity as the beloved Son was made known and his mission to save the world was inaugurated. Let us ask God during our prayer to help us be faithful as we continue Jesus' saving mission in our world today . . .

Prayer

God of love, you are pleased to announce the Presence of your beloved Son. Help us to be faithful in announcing his Presence to all those we meet and to be pleasing to you in all we do. We ask this through Christ our Lord. **Amen**.

Gospel (Matt 3:13-17)

Jesus came from Galilee to John at the Jordan to be baptized by him. John tried to prevent him, saying, "I need to be baptized by you, and yet you are coming to me?" Jesus said to him in reply, "Allow it now, for thus it is fitting for us to fulfill all righteousness." Then he allowed him. After Jesus was baptized, he came up from the water and behold, the heavens were opened for him, and he saw the Spirit of God descending like a dove and coming upon him. And a voice came from the heavens, saying, "This is my beloved Son, with whom I am well pleased."

Brief Silence

For Reflection

Jesus comes to John, who is baptizing in the River Jordan. John is pointing to a baptism greater than his and to a person greater than he. Jesus asks John to baptize him in order to "fulfill all righteousness" and thus show forth his continuity with the tradition in which John stands. But more happens. When the heavens open, the Spirit descends and Jesus is announced as the "beloved Son," a new tradition is born, and humanity's relationship with God is changed forever. We who are baptized into Christ become God's beloved sons and daughters and God is "well pleased" with us, too, when we are faithful to our relationship with God and to each other. Through baptism we are invited into this new tradition. Baptism inaugurates us into a Spirit-filled tradition where a new covenantal relationship with God becomes possible. We are invited into a union with God's "beloved Son" that confers on us his identity, his going "about doing good," his intimate relationship with his Father. We cannot take our baptism for granted because it is not simply a ritual that happens and is finished, but it is a relationship and way of life to be lived.

✦ Baptized into Christ, I am God's "beloved," and the difference this makes in how I live and minister is . . .

Brief Silence

Prayer

God of love, you desire to have an intimate relationship with us and are well pleased when we respond to your love with our love. May we always be grateful for your gift of Life and love, for your gift of the divine Son, and for loving us into fullness of Life. We ask this through Christ our Lord. **Amen**.

John the Baptist testifies about who he has come to know Jesus to be. Let us prepare ourselves for our reflection and prayer so we may come to know this Jesus more intimately . . .

Prayer

Father in heaven, you sent your Spirit to rest upon your beloved Son at his baptism. Help us to be like John the Baptist, who recognized Jesus as the great One sent from you to baptize us with the Holy Spirit. We ask this through Christ our Lord. **Amen**.

Gospel (John 1:29-34)

John the Baptist saw Jesus coming toward him and said, "Behold, the Lamb of God, who takes away the sin of the world. He is the one of whom I said, 'A man is coming after me who ranks ahead of me because he existed before me.' I did not know him, but the reason why I came baptizing with water was that he might be made known to Israel." John testified further, saying, "I saw the Spirit come down like a dove from heaven and remain upon him. I did not know him, but the one who sent me to baptize with water told me, 'On whomever you see the Spirit come down and remain, he is the one who will baptize with the Holy Spirit.' Now I have seen and testified that he is the Son of God."

Brief Silence

For Reflection

This gospel is a testimony of what John has come to know about who Jesus is: Lamb of God, One who forgives sins, One who pre-exists, One who is Spirit-filled, One who baptizes with the Holy Spirit, Son of God. But John's testimony does not exhaust the richness of Jesus' identity; there is even more. John the Baptist unveils in his relationship to Christ the posture of the church, which is to go from not knowing to seeing to testifying. We don't come to a one-time understanding of Christ. Our whole lives are spent beholding the Lamb of God, and in this very encounter we receive the Spirit and are commissioned to carry on Jesus' saving mission. The surprise of this gospel is that, as the Father entrusted to the beloved Son the work of salvation, by baptizing us with the Holy Spirit Jesus entrusts *to us* this same saving mission. The mystery of who Jesus is continues to be revealed to us and through us today. What more are we discovering? What more are we revealing? Is Jesus more than a passerby to us?

✦ As I look on the faces of those coming to receive Holy Communion, I discover this about Jesus . . .

Brief Silence

Prayer
Revealing God, you sent the Spirit of your risen Son to dwell within us and enable us to continue his saving mission. Be with us always as we strive to recognize him in those around us, as we strive to be faithful as he was, as we ask him to guide us in all things. We ask this through Christ our Lord. **Amen**.

At this very moment, in the midst of our daily struggles and joys, Jesus calls us to follow him. Let us hear God's call and ask for the grace to follow more faithfully . . .

Prayer

Gracious God, your Son Jesus called forth followers to minister with him in bringing salvation to all people. Open us to hear that same call and help us to be faithful as we continue his saving mission. We ask this through Christ our Lord. **Amen**.

Gospel (Matt 4:12-23)

When Jesus heard that John had been arrested, he withdrew to Galilee. He left Nazareth and went to live in Capernaum by the sea, in the region of Zebulun and Naphtali, that what had been said through Isaiah the prophet might be fulfilled: / *Land of Zebulun and land of Naphtali, / the way to the sea, beyond the Jordan, / Galilee of the Gentiles, / the people who sit in darkness have seen a great light, / on those dwelling in a land overshadowed by death / light has arisen.* / From that time on, Jesus began to preach and say, "Repent, for the kingdom of heaven is at hand."

As he was walking by the Sea of Galilee, he saw two brothers, Simon who is called Peter, and his brother Andrew, casting a net into the sea; they were fishermen. He said to them, "Come after me, and I will make you fishers of men." At once they left their nets and followed him. He walked along from there and saw two other brothers, James, the son of Zebedee, and his brother John. They were in a boat, with their father Zebedee, mending their nets. He called them, and immediately they left their boat and their father and followed him. He went around all of Galilee, teaching in their synagogues, proclaiming the gospel of the kingdom, and curing every disease and illness among the people.

Brief Silence

For Reflection

At the beginning of Jesus' public ministry, the mystery of what he is about is revealed: something new is happening. Jesus has a command about him, a persona, an immense Presence that brings forth response. Jesus calls Peter and Andrew, James and John to leave their life as they knew it and become disciples who now proclaim the "gospel of the kingdom." Humanity moves now from darkness into "a great light." New teaching happens now. New healing comes now. New Life is given now. Now, a new Presence. To recognize this "kingdom of heaven" in our midst invites us to enter ever more fully into God's reign by following Jesus. The good news is that the light begins shining here—among the Gentiles, in the darkness. The call of disciples is to be here—in the darkness. The way out of a dark and condemned land is to hear Jesus' call to follow him. We cannot hear it often enough, for this is the way to living in the light. This is how God's kingdom is established: faithful disciples hear Jesus' call, repent, and faithfully follow. In this way gloom and darkness are overcome.

✦ Living the spirituality of my ministry helps others experience the Presence of Christ in their daily living when I . . .

Brief Silence

Prayer

God of light, you sent the Light of your divine Son to break through the darkness of our own unfaithfulness and call us to a new life of answering Jesus' call to bring salvation to all. Accompany us on our life journey and help us to hear and be faithful to whatever Jesus' call asks of us. We ask this through Christ our Lord. **Amen.**

When Jesus is presented in the temple, Simeon and Anna recognize him as the long-awaited Messiah. As we spend some time in reflection and prayer, may we grow in our own willingness to encounter the Messiah who is ever in our midst . . .

Prayer

O God of light and goodness, you sent your only-begotten Son into the world to be our Light and our salvation. Help us open ourselves more perfectly to the Holy Spirit who enables us to be that Light for others. We ask this through Christ our Lord. **Amen**.

Gospel (Luke 2:22-32 [Longer Form: Luke 2:22-40])

When the days were completed for their purification according to the law of Moses, / Mary and Joseph took Jesus up to Jerusalem to present him to the Lord, / just as it is written in the law of the Lord, *Every male that opens the womb shall be consecrated to the Lord,* and to offer the sacrifice of *a pair of turtledoves or two young pigeons,* in accordance with the dictate in the law of the Lord.

Now there was a man in Jerusalem whose name was Simeon. This man was righteous and devout, awaiting the consolation of Israel, and the Holy Spirit was upon him. It had been revealed to him by the Holy Spirit that he should not see death before he had seen the Christ of the Lord. He came in the Spirit into the temple; and when the parents brought in the child Jesus to perform the custom of the law in regard to him, he took him into his arms and blessed God, saying: / "Now, Master, you may let your servant go / in peace, according to your word, / for my eyes have seen your salvation, / which you prepared in sight of all the peoples, / a light for revelation to the Gentiles, / and glory for your people Israel."

Brief Silence

For Reflection

Mary and Joseph were faithful to the law when they came to present their forty-day-old Son in the temple and offer the pre-scribed sacrifice. But what happened in his life went far beyond the expectations of the law. "The child grew and became strong, filled with wisdom; and the favor of God was upon him." This is the same sentiment expressed in Luke's gospel about Jesus, for the next time it is recorded that Jesus is in the temple is when he was twelve years old: "And Jesus advanced [in] wisdom and age and favor before God and man" (Luke 2:52, NABRE). Jesus grew in the Spirit; so must we. It is Simeon and Anna who show us that more is necessary than obedience to the law in order to grow in the Spirit and recognize the presence of the Son-Messiah. Filled with expectation, they were actively waiting and looking for "the Christ of the Lord" and the "redemption of Jerusalem." Their very expectation and waiting was the work of the Holy Spirit within them. As with Simeon and Anna, our own lives must be filled with the expectation and waiting that is truly the work of the Holy Spirit within us. Only then will we see and recognize the Messiah in our midst.

✦ The Holy Spirit leads me to encounter the Messiah in those coming to me to receive Holy Communion when I . . .

Brief Silence

Prayer

Blessed are you, Lord God, who sent the Light of the World into our midst to bring us a new revelation of redemption. Stir in our hearts gratitude for the gift of Light and salvation and help us to yearn deeply and await faithfully for the fullness of Life eternal. We ask this through Christ our Lord. **Amen**.

Jesus calls his disciples to be salt of the earth and light of the world. Let us ask for the grace to be faithful to our discipleship . . .

Prayer

O God, your divine Son is the Light that shines on us which enables us to follow him in his saving ministry with faithfulness and eagerness. Strengthen us that our light might shine forth and bring good to others. We ask this through Christ our Lord. **Amen**.

Gospel (Matt 5:13-16)

Jesus said to his disciples: "You are the salt of the earth. But if salt loses its taste, with what can it be seasoned? It is no longer good for anything but to be thrown out and trampled underfoot. You are the light of the world. A city set on a mountain cannot be hidden. Nor do they light a lamp and then put it under a bushel basket; it is set on a lampstand, where it gives light to all in the house. Just so, your light must shine before others, that they may see your good deeds and glorify your heavenly Father."

Brief Silence

For Reflection

Jesus uses salt and light in this gospel to describe qualities of disciples, two metaphors with both positive and negative import. Salt enhances, but is thrown away and trampled if it becomes tasteless. Light shines, but is ineffective if it is hidden. Jesus is clearly saying that disciples must spend themselves in preserving and carrying forward his saving mission. Disciples must season the world with God's word and faithfully shine forth God's Presence. The choice is ours: to season or be discarded, to shine or be hidden. Salt is the bridge between who we are and the good we do. Salt brings out and enhances what is already there—the God-given good within us. Salt is the power Jesus gives his disciples to preserve and carry forward his saving work. Light is the insight the Holy Spirit gives to disciples to know the truth of the Gospel and devise ways to help others grasp Jesus' way of living. It is light that shines forth from us, a Light that is the Presence of the risen Christ himself within us.

✦ Situations in my life that could use "salt" are . . . that need "light" are . . .

Brief Silence

Prayer
Our life, O God, is in your hands. It is you who helps us to shine forth the Presence of your divine Son. Be with us as we strive to be ever more faithful to his Gospel that brings salt and light to our world. We ask this through Christ our Lord. **Amen**.

Jesus calls us to grasp that the fundamental meaning of keeping God's law is to strive for righteous relationships with each other and God. Let us consider when we have fallen short of loving others and seek God's mercy . . .

Prayer

O God, your Law is written in our hearts so that we might know how to live as your Son taught us. Help us to go beyond the letter of the law and live in your Spirit, bringing goodness and truth to all we meet. We ask this through Christ our Lord. **Amen**.

Gospel (Matt 5:20-22a, 27-28, 33-34a, 37
[Longer Form: Matt 5:17-37])

Jesus said to his disciples: "I tell you, unless your righteousness surpasses that of the scribes and Pharisees, you will not enter the kingdom of heaven.

"You have heard that it was said to your ancestors, *You shall not kill; and whoever kills will be liable to judgment.* But I say to you, whoever is angry with his brother will be liable to judgment.

"You have heard that it was said, *You shall not commit adultery.* But I say to you, everyone who looks at a woman with lust has already committed adultery with her in his heart.

"Again you have heard that it was said to your ancestors, *Do not take a false oath, but make good to the Lord all that you vow.* But I say to you, do not swear at all. Let your 'Yes' mean 'Yes,' and your 'No' mean 'No.' Anything more is from the evil one."

Brief Silence

For Reflection

In this gospel selection, a continuation of Jesus' Sermon on the Mount which is a blueprint for faithful Christian living, Jesus is speaking about laws and human behavior. He does not make his hearers' lives easier by easing the law; he does give a better reason for keeping it than the consequences of breaking laws: deepening right relationships with those around us. He has not come to abolish the law; he has come to show us what its fulfillment looks like. What does it mean for Jesus to fulfill the law? Jesus sees in the law the means to the fulfillment of time ("until all things have taken place"), when the law will be replaced by righteous relationships within the kingdom of heaven. The fundamental law is gift of self to others. When self-giving is lacking in any act of keeping the law, the law in fact is not kept. We are to keep the law as the way to enter a manner of caring for and relating to others that leads to fullness of Life. Our model for so doing is Jesus.

✦ Jesus fulfilled the law; I fulfill the law when I . . .

Brief Silence

Prayer

God of an everlasting kingdom, your law is goodness and truth. Be with us as we strive to do your will and come to the fullness of your Life. We ask this through Christ our Lord. **Amen**.

Jesus challenges us to go beyond an eye for an eye, to love our enemies, to go the extra mile. Let us ask during our prayer for the grace to do as Jesus asks and seek forgiveness for the times we have failed . . .

Prayer

Loving God, you teach us to care for others with the same care you have shown us. Help us to love with your all-embracing love and to welcome into our care and concern everyone whom we encounter. We ask this through Christ our Lord. **Amen**.

Gospel (Matt 5:38-48)

Jesus said to his disciples: "You have heard that it was said, *An eye for an eye and a tooth for a tooth.* But I say to you, offer no resistance to one who is evil. When someone strikes you on your right cheek, turn the other one as well. If anyone wants to go to law with you over your tunic, hand over your cloak as well. Should anyone press you into service for one mile, go for two miles. Give to the one who asks of you, and do not turn your back on one who wants to borrow.

"You have heard that it was said, *You shall love your neighbor and hate your enemy.* But I say to you, love your enemies and pray for those who persecute you, that you may be children of your heavenly Father, for he makes his sun rise on the bad and the good, and causes rain to fall on the just and the unjust. For if you love those who love you, what recompense will you have? Do not the tax collectors do the same? And if you greet your brothers only, what is unusual about that? Do not the pagans do the same? So be perfect, just as your heavenly Father is perfect."

Brief Silence

For Reflection

Jesus challenges us to go beyond our expected responses to human interactions. We are to offer no resistance to those who do us harm, give more than is asked of us, love our enemies—a tall order in itself! Surely this approaches "perfect" behavior. Most of us would be quite happy with our lives if we could even put this much of Jesus' teaching into practice! But, challenging as they are, his examples of this "beyond" are nonetheless still finite human actions and limited love. In both Greek and Latin vocabulary, "perfect" has to do with bringing to completion, fulfillment, having an ultimate end in sight. In this sense, all our human actions are finite and limited. Even going the extra mile is still just one more mile. Giving our coat to another is still just a coat. Jesus is asking us to stop thinking in terms of measurements and begin acting in terms of how our heavenly Father treats us. God's graces are showered upon all; God's care is extended to all; God's love is poured forth upon all. But most of all, God's Son loved with his all. He showed us what "perfect" is: he gave himself. Again and again.

✦ I am challenged to go beyond my finite human actions and limited love when . . .

Brief Silence

Prayer

O God of limitless love and care, you are perfect beyond all measure. Help us to live our lives by not counting the cost, but by keeping before us the limitless self-giving of your divine Son. We ask this through Christ our Lord. **Amen**.

Jesus teaches us not to worry unduly about the things of this life, but to trust wholeheartedly in God's care for us. As we begin our prayer and reflection, let us seek the mercy of this loving God . . .

Prayer

Loving God, you ask us to serve you and you alone. Help us to have undivided hearts turned toward your love, mercy, forgiveness, peace, and justice. We ask this through Christ our Lord. **Amen**.

Gospel (Matt 6:24-34)

Jesus said to his disciples: "No one can serve two masters. He will either hate one and love the other, or be devoted to one and despise the other. You cannot serve God and mammon.

"Therefore I tell you, do not worry about your life, what you will eat or drink, or about your body, what you will wear. Is not life more than food and the body more than clothing? Look at the birds in the sky; they do not sow or reap, they gather nothing into barns, yet your heavenly Father feeds them. Are not you more important than they? Can any of you by worrying add a single moment to your life-span? Why are you anxious about clothes? Learn from the way the wild flowers grow. They do not work or spin. But I tell you that not even Solomon in all his splendor was clothed like one of them. If God so clothes the grass of the field, which grows today and is thrown into the oven tomorrow, will he not much more provide for you, O you of little faith? So do not worry and say, 'What are we to eat?' or 'What are we to drink?' or 'What are we to wear?' All these things the pagans seek. Your heavenly Father knows that you need them all. But seek first the kingdom of God and his righteousness, and all these things will be given you besides. Do not worry about tomorrow; tomorrow will take care of itself. Sufficient for a day is its own evil."

Brief Silence

For Reflection

Telling humans not to worry about tomorrow is like telling them not to be the center of their own lives. And that is exactly the point of this gospel! The two masters are God or ourselves. Yes, we ourselves are the mammon. And it is much harder to detect serving ourselves as mammon than mammon as money or material things (its usual meaning). When we become fixated on material things—the latest electronic gadget, a certain TV show that controls our time schedule, any kind of addiction—we have something specific "out there" to examine, judge, change. But when we worry and become fixated on ourselves, the behavior is much more difficult to detect, face, and overcome. If we choose God, the center of our lives shifts from ourselves to God then to others. Worrying draws us into ourselves; caring for others draws us out of ourselves. If we choose God, we will feed on God's generosity, be clothed in God's gift of Life, and be made rich in faith. This choice is sufficient not only for a day, but for a whole lifetime—even for all eternity.

✦ Choosing God over myself and material things has gifted me with . . .

Brief Silence

Prayer

Loving God, you free us from anxiety and worry when we turn ourselves toward you. Help us to become more completely aware of your abiding Presence to us and to let you guide us in caring for others as you care for us. We ask this through Christ our Lord. **Amen**.

Lent is a time of self-examination and conversion. Let us open ourselves during our reflection and prayer to hear God calling us to repentance and mercy.

Prayer

Merciful and gracious God, you give us the help and strength of your grace. May our Lent be fruitful and may we come to celebrate the fullness of Easter joy. We ask this through Christ our Lord. **Amen**.

Gospel (Matt 6:1-6, 16-18)

Jesus said to his disciples: "Take care not to perform righteous deeds in order that people may see them; otherwise, you will have no recompense from your heavenly Father. When you give alms, do not blow a trumpet before you, as the hypocrites do in the synagogues and in the streets to win the praise of others. Amen, I say to you, they have received their reward. But when you give alms, do not let your left hand know what your right is doing, so that your almsgiving may be secret. And your Father who sees in secret will repay you.

"When you pray, do not be like the hypocrites, who love to stand and pray in the synagogues and on street corners so that others may see them. Amen, I say to you, they have received their reward. But when you pray, go to your inner room, close the door, and pray to your Father in secret. And your Father who sees in secret will repay you.

"When you fast, do not look gloomy like the hypocrites. They neglect their appearance, so that they may appear to others to be fasting. Amen, I say to you, they have received their reward. But when you fast, anoint your head and wash your face, so that you may not appear to be fasting, except to your Father who is hidden. And your Father who sees what is hidden will repay you."

Brief Silence

For Reflection

Penance is one Lenten practice that helps us and nourishes us, preparing us to receive the new Life that Easter promises. The penance of Lent is necessary to *change us* and to reorient us toward God. And by changing ourselves, we change our relationship to God and each other. Lent is necessary so that the pieces of our lives can be anchored in the God who is merciful and forgiving, promising us a fresh start every time we turn to God for guidance. Lent is a time to renew ourselves so that we can live faithfully in Christ.

Jesus tells us how *not* to "perform righteous deeds": not to do them to receive the praise of others and be immediately rewarded. He also tells us *how* to do Lenten penance: to do it "in secret" and receive lasting repayment from God. The heart of Lenten penance is the hard work of opening ourselves to God's transforming grace. This is internal work that bears external effects. What is to be seen is not the penance we do, but the fruit of penance that is the grace of God at work in us. In this way is the desert of our lives turned into fertile soil anchored by the very Life of God.

✦ The fruits of my penance that I hope to see by the end of Lent are . . .

Brief Silence

Prayer

God of Life, you offer us new Life during this special Lenten time of renewal and conversion. Be with us on our Lenten journey and lead us to the fullness of Life to come. We ask this through Christ our Lord. **Amen**.

As we begin Lent, we are warned about the dangers of temptation that lead to sin. Let us acknowledge during our prayer that we have given in to temptation and seek God's mercy . . .

Prayer

Forgiving God, you know that we humans are weak and give in to temptations. Strengthen us when we face evil and help us always to look to you for guidance in our decisions and actions. We ask this through Christ our Lord. **Amen**.

Gospel (Matt 4:1-11)

At that time Jesus was led by the Spirit into the desert to be tempted by the devil. He fasted for forty days and forty nights, and afterwards he was hungry. The tempter approached and said to him, "If you are the Son of God, command that these stones become loaves of bread." He said in reply, "It is written: / *One does not live on bread alone, / but on every word that comes forth / from the mouth of God."*

Then the devil took him to the holy city, and made him stand on the parapet of the temple, and said to him, "If you are the Son of God, throw yourself down. For it is written: / *He will command his angels concerning you / and with their hands they will support you, / lest you dash your foot against a stone."* / Jesus answered him, "Again it is written, *You shall not put the Lord, your God, to the test."* Then the devil took him up to a very high mountain, and showed him all the kingdoms of the world in their magnificence, and he said to him, "All these I shall give to you, if you will prostrate yourself and worship me." At this, Jesus said to him, "Get away, Satan! It is written: / *The Lord, your God, shall you worship / and him alone shall you serve."*

Then the devil left him and, behold, angels came and ministered to him.

Brief Silence

For Reflection

Jesus walked every aspect of our human journey, even submitting himself to temptation and death. At the end of his desert experience, he would have been hungry, would have sought companionship, would have been wanting a shower and haircut. After forty days alone in the desert, Jesus was vulnerable, was ripe for temptation, was ripe to be led where under other circumstances he might not have gone. So the devil was smart; he knew how to hit Jesus where he was most vulnerable; he tried to allure him with tantalizing temptations. This gospel story teaches us that temptation comes most surely when we are most vulnerable. Temptation is essentially an enticement to put our own desires and needs first, to do what we think is best for ourselves at the moment, to give in to our impulses without considering too seriously the consequences. Resisting temptation, then, is really a matter of resisting self-centeredness. Like Jesus, we must choose instead to surrender ourselves to God who alone should be the center of our lives. To make any other choice is to choose a false god. This First Sunday of Lent poses this question: Do we serve god or God?

✦ I am a living "Eucharist" (nourishment) for those struggling with temptations whenever I . . .

Brief Silence

Prayer

Merciful God, you are with us even when we give in to temptations and stray from your loving embrace. During this Lent help us to turn ourselves from our own self-centeredness and focus more faithfully on you and your divine Presence, guiding us in all things. We ask this through Christ our Lord. **Amen.**

Jesus took Peter, James, and John up to a mountaintop and was transfigured in glory before them. As we repent of our sinfulness during our prayer and reflection, let us welcome God's mercy as a share in Jesus' glory . . .

Prayer

Glorious God, you allowed Peter, James, and John to witness the dazzling brightness of the transfigured Jesus. Through our good actions we undertake for others, help us to witness that same glory in the joy of others. We ask this through Christ our Lord. **Amen**.

Gospel (Matt 17:1-9)

Jesus took Peter, James, and John his brother, and led them up a high mountain by themselves. And he was transfigured before them; his face shone like the sun and his clothes became white as light. And behold, Moses and Elijah appeared to them, conversing with him. Then Peter said to Jesus in reply, "Lord, it is good that we are here. If you wish, I will make three tents here, one for you, one for Moses, and one for Elijah." While he was still speaking, behold, a bright cloud cast a shadow over them, then from the cloud came a voice that said, "This is my beloved Son, with whom I am well pleased; listen to him." When the disciples heard this, they fell prostrate and were very much afraid. But Jesus came and touched them, saying, "Rise, and do not be afraid." And when the disciples raised their eyes, they saw no one else but Jesus alone.

As they were coming down from the mountain, Jesus charged them, "Do not tell the vision to anyone until the Son of Man has been raised from the dead."

Brief Silence

For Reflection

Listening to Jesus does more than promise glory; it reminds us that to reach that glory we must be willing to join Jesus in his passion and death as well. Our Christian journey is about listening to God's word, living a life of dying to self, and basking in the new Life which comes to those who faithfully follow Jesus "up a high mountain" of transfiguration and promised glory and also "down from the mountain" to the everyday temptations and the demands of self-giving. Why are we willing to travel this Christian journey, to climb arduous mountains to be given the blessing of glory? What high mountain must we climb for us to witness Jesus' transfiguration? We must climb the high mountain of listening to Jesus, the high mountain of being pleasing to him, the high mountain of opening ourselves to the touch of his Presence. When we climb this mountain, we forsake our own agenda of pitching the tent of satisfaction with our own works to enter into the glory of the Life Jesus offers us. The mountain is steep; the climb is ours to choose; the vision at the top is divine—"white as light," shining "like the sun." Can we see him?

✦ I see Jesus' transfigured glory in the faces of those who come to receive Holy Communion and this moves me to . . .

Brief Silence

Prayer

You teach us through Jesus, God our Father, that the way to glory is through the cross. Help us to listen to him, to live his Gospel with rigor, and to embrace the Lenten penance that brings us to conversion of heart and the promise of sharing in everlasting glory with you. We ask this through Christ our Lord. **Amen**.

Jesus' encounter with the Samaritan woman at the well leads her to believe in him as the "savior of the world." As we settle ourselves into a time of prayer and reflection, may we seek God's mercy for the times we have not been open to encountering Jesus . . .

Prayer

Gracious God, your Son is the living water that brings us Life and faithfulness. Help us to drink deeply of this water that we might live the Gospel with ever more fervent fidelity. We ask this through Christ our Lord. **Amen**.

Gospel (John 4:5-15, 19b-26, 39a, 40-42
[Longer Form: John 4:5-42])

Jesus came to a town of Samaria called Sychar, near the plot of land that Jacob had given to his son Joseph. Jacob's well was there. Jesus, tired from his journey, sat down there at the well. It was about noon.

A woman of Samaria came to draw water. Jesus said to her, "Give me a drink." His disciples had gone into the town to buy food. The Samaritan woman said to him, "How can you, a Jew, ask me, a Samaritan woman, for a drink?"—For Jews use nothing in common with Samaritans.—Jesus answered and said to her, "If you knew the gift of God and who is saying to you, 'Give me a drink,' you would have asked him and he would have given you living water." The woman said to him, "Sir, you do not even have a bucket and the cistern is deep; where then can you get this living water? Are you greater than our father Jacob, who gave us this cistern and drank from it himself with his children and his flocks?" Jesus answered and said to her, "Everyone who drinks this water will be thirsty again; but whoever drinks the water I shall give will never thirst; the water I shall give will become in him a spring of water welling up to eternal life." The woman said to him, "Sir, give me this water, so that I may not be thirsty or have to keep coming here to draw water.

"I can see that you are a prophet. Our ancestors worshiped on this mountain; but you people say that the place to worship is in Jerusalem." Jesus said to her, "Believe me, woman, the hour is coming when you will worship the Father neither on this mountain nor in Jerusalem. You people worship what you do not understand; we worship what we understand, because salvation is from the Jews. But the hour is coming, and is now here, when true worshipers will worship the Father in Spirit and truth; and indeed the Father seeks such people to worship him. God is Spirit, and those who worship him must worship in Spirit and truth." The woman said to him, "I know that the Messiah is coming, the one called the Christ; when he comes, he will tell us everything." Jesus said to her, "I am he, the one who is speaking with you."

Many of the Samaritans of that town began to believe in him. When the Samaritans came to him, they invited him to stay with them; and he stayed there two days. Many more began to believe in him because of his word, and they said to the woman, "We no longer believe because of your word; for we have heard for ourselves, and we know that this is truly the savior of the world."

Brief Silence

For Reflection

When Jesus asked the Samaritan woman for a drink of water, she
completely misunderstood what Jesus was really asking: to understand the "gift of God" already given to her. What he was offering her was the gift of his very Self: the living water that would
lead her from chance meeting to divine encounter, from being a
woman who attempts to deceive Jesus ("I do not have a husband")
to becoming one who gives true testimony to "the Christ," from
her expectation of the Messiah to her belief that the "savior of the
world" has come. True encounters with Jesus never leave anyone
the same. Instead of a woman at a well to draw water (a simple,
daily, necessary task), she becomes a disciple-woman who testifies to her townsfolk about her life-changing encounter (a lifelong
mystery to be lived). Our life, too, unfolds in simple scenes fraught
with this same immense potential to come to recognize who Jesus
is and be changed by him. Jesus is the "gift of God" who gives us
the "living water" of his own preaching, dying, and rising. All we
need to do is drink deeply and we, too, will never thirst again, will
live forever.

✦ I have encountered Jesus when . . . These encounters have
transformed me in these ways . . .

Brief Silence

Prayer

God of Life and goodness, you give us this time of Lent to renew
ourselves and prepare to recommit ourselves to our baptismal
promises. Strengthen us in our resolve to see ourselves for who we
are and be transformed into ever more perfect Presences of your
risen Son. We ask this through Christ our Lord. Amen.

Jesus re-creates the man born blind not only by giving him sight, but by bringing him to be a believing disciple. Let us open ourselves to Jesus' healing touch during our prayer and ask him to re-create us through his mercy and forgiveness . . .

Prayer

All-knowing God, you see into our hearts and know when we harbor doubt and fear, insight and deep faith. May we always be washed clean of whatever keeps us from seeing and believing in your saving Presence and love. We ask this through Christ our Lord. **Amen**.

Gospel (John 9:1, 6-9, 13-17, 34-38 [Longer Form: John 9:1-41])

As Jesus passed by he saw a man blind from birth. He spat on the ground and made clay with the saliva, and smeared the clay on his eyes, and said to him, "Go wash in the Pool of Siloam"—which means Sent—. So he went and washed, and came back able to see.

His neighbors and those who had seen him earlier as a beggar said, "Isn't this the one who used to sit and beg?" Some said, "It is," but others said, "No, he just looks like him." He said, "I am."

They brought the one who was once blind to the Pharisees. Now Jesus had made clay and opened his eyes on a sabbath. So then the Pharisees also asked him how he was able to see. He said to them, "He put clay on my eyes, and I washed, and now I can see." So some of the Pharisees said, "This man is not from God, because he does not keep the sabbath." But others said, "How can a sinful man do such signs?" And there was a division among them. So they said to the blind man again, "What do you have to say about him, since he opened your eyes?" He said, "He is a prophet."

They answered and said to him, "You were born totally in sin, and are you trying to teach us?" Then they threw him out.

When Jesus heard that they had thrown him out, he found him and said, "Do you believe in the Son of Man?" He answered and said, "Who is he, sir, that I may believe in him?" Jesus said to him, "You have seen him, and the one speaking with you is he." He said, "I do believe, Lord," and he worshiped him.

Brief Silence

For Reflection

In making clay from his own saliva and smearing it on the blind man's eyes, Jesus re-creates the man by transferring something of his own being to the man. Healed, the man is not afraid to own up to his being the one Jesus touched with clay and spittle. This healed man is now united with Jesus in a new way. The man is anointed by Jesus and comes to be a stalwart, believing disciple. Even in the face of controversy and pounding questions, the healed man does not back down from his intimate connection with Jesus. Not even the powerful Pharisees can sway him from his testimony to the work of Jesus in him.

In baptism we, too, encounter Jesus and become a new creation in him. And we are re-created each time we encounter something of God. Our entire lives of faithful discipleship are a matter of allowing God to touch us with something of the divine Self, opening ourselves to God's healing anointing, becoming ever more perfectly who God desires us to be: faithful followers of the divine Son.

✦ My daily living witnesses to my belief that receiving Jesus in Holy Communion re-creates who I am in him when . . .

Brief Silence

Prayer

Wondrous God, you are the divine Creator and yet you care enough for us to send your Son to touch us and heal us of all alienation. Help our unbelief, O God. Bring us to be sure witnesses of your risen Son. We ask this through Christ our Lord. **Amen**.

Jesus calls Lazarus forth from death to life. Let us rid ourselves of distractions during our prayer and reflection and become more attentive to God's Presence so that we, too, might come to new Life . . .

Prayer

"Lazarus, come out!" Jesus cries out and, Father of Life, you brought forth Lazarus from death to new life. Help us to hear Jesus call to us to come closer to him and receive the Life only you can offer. We ask this through Christ our Lord. **Amen**.

Gospel (John 11:3-7, 17, 20-27, 33b-45
[Longer Form: John 11:1-45])

The sisters of Lazarus sent word to Jesus, saying, "Master, the one you love is ill." When Jesus heard this he said, "This illness is not to end in death, but is for the glory of God, that the Son of God may be glorified through it." Now Jesus loved Martha and her sister and Lazarus. So when he heard that he was ill, he remained for two days in the place where he was. Then after this he said to his disciples, "Let us go back to Judea."

When Jesus arrived, he found that Lazarus had already been in the tomb for four days. When Martha heard that Jesus was coming, she went to meet him; but Mary sat at home. Martha said to Jesus, "Lord, if you had been here, my brother would not have died. But even now I know that whatever you ask of God, God will give you." Jesus said to her, "Your brother will rise." Martha said, "I know he will rise, in the resurrection on the last day." Jesus told her, "I am the resurrection and the life; whoever believes in me, even if he dies, will live, and everyone who lives and believes in me will never die. Do you believe this?" She said to him, "Yes,

Lord. I have come to believe that you are the Christ, the Son of God, the one who is coming into the world."

He became perturbed and deeply troubled, and said, "Where have you laid him?" They said to him, "Sir, come and see." And Jesus wept. So the Jews said, "See how he loved him." But some of them said, "Could not the one who opened the eyes of the blind man have done something so that this man would not have died?"

So Jesus, perturbed again, came to the tomb. It was a cave, and a stone lay across it. Jesus said, "Take away the stone." Martha, the dead man's sister, said to him, "Lord, by now there will be a stench; he has been dead for four days." Jesus said to her, "Did I not tell you that if you believe you will see the glory of God?" So they took away the stone. And Jesus raised his eyes and said, "Father, I thank you for hearing me. I know that you always hear me; but because of the crowd here I have said this, that they may believe that you sent me." And when he had said this, he cried out in a loud voice, "Lazarus, come out!" The dead man came out, tied hand and foot with burial bands, and his face was wrapped in a cloth. So Jesus said to them, "Untie him and let him go."

Now many of the Jews who had come to Mary and seen what he had done began to believe in him.

Brief Silence

For Reflection

Both Martha and Mary are deeply agitated when Jesus does not arrive until after Lazarus is dead and buried. What could Jesus do for the dead? They express great conviction in Jesus' healing power: "Lord, if you had been here, my brother would not have died." Their conviction, however, was tied to their human experience of the fragility of sickness and the finality of death. Believing that Jesus could perform miracles did not prepare them for the astonishing revelation that he had power over death itself. Jesus' action surmounts human experience and reveals something entirely new: "everyone who lives and believes in [him] will never die." Belief in Jesus unties us from the limits of human experience and frees us for the eternity of risen Life. This gospel event clearly has implications beyond Lazarus' return to life and bringing the crowd to belief. First of all, Lazarus' death and being brought back to life foreshadows Jesus' and our journey from death to Life. Even as amazing as the raising of Lazarus is, the full extent of Jesus' power over death would be revealed only in his resurrection and in ours.

✦ My belief in Jesus looks like . . . To never die means to me . . .

Brief Silence

Prayer

Such sorrow of heart we have, dear God, when we face the death of a loved one! Be with us as we struggle to believe in your power over death and help us journey faithfully toward that fullness of Life which conquers death and brings untold joy. We ask this through Christ our Lord. **Amen**.

We commemorate Jesus' triumphant entry into Jerusalem and reflect on his passion story. Let us resolve to spend this Holy Week in prayer and reflection as much as we are able and open ourselves to God's saving mystery . . .

Prayer

May we hear in this passion account, heavenly Father, your Son's great love for us, a love so all-embracing that he willingly accepted suffering and death. Open our hearts to the wondrous mystery we celebrate this Holy Week and through our prayer lead us to the joy of the resurrection. We ask this through Christ our Lord. **Amen**.

Gospel (Matt 27:11-54 [Longer Form: Matt 26:14–27:66])

Jesus stood before the governor, Pontius Pilate, who questioned him, "Are you the king of the Jews?" Jesus said, "You say so." And when he was accused by the chief priests and elders, he made no answer. Then Pilate said to him, "Do you not hear how many things they are testifying against you?" But he did not answer him one word, so that the governor was greatly amazed.

Now on the occasion of the feast the governor was accustomed to release to the crowd one prisoner whom they wished. And at that time they had a notorious prisoner called Barabbas. So when they had assembled, Pilate said to them, "Which one do you want me to release to you, Barabbas, or Jesus called Christ?" For he knew that it was out of envy that they had handed him over. While he was still seated on the bench, his wife sent him a message, "Have nothing to do with that righteous man. I suffered much in a dream today because of him." The chief priests and the elders persuaded the crowds to ask for Barabbas but to destroy Jesus. The governor said to them in reply, "Which of the two do you want me to release to you?" They answered, "Barabbas!" Pilate said to them, "Then what shall I do with Jesus called Christ?" They all said, "Let him be crucified!" But he said, "Why? What evil has he done?" They only shouted the louder, "Let him be crucified!" When Pilate saw that he was not succeeding at all, but that a riot was breaking out instead, he took water and washed his hands in the sight of the crowd, saying, "I am innocent of this man's blood. Look to it yourselves." And the whole people said in reply, "His blood be upon us and upon our children." Then he released Barabbas to them, but after he had Jesus scourged, he handed him over to be crucified.

Then the soldiers of the governor took Jesus inside the praetorium and gathered the whole cohort around him. They stripped off his clothes and threw a scarlet military cloak about him. Weaving a crown out of thorns, they placed it on his head, and a reed in his right hand. And kneeling before him, they mocked him, saying, "Hail, King of the Jews!" They spat upon him and took the reed and kept striking him on the head. And when they had mocked him, they stripped him of the cloak, dressed him in his own clothes, and led him off to crucify him.

As they were going out, they met a Cyrenian named Simon; this man they pressed into service to carry his cross.

And when they came to a place called Golgotha—which means Place of the Skull—, they gave Jesus wine to drink mixed with gall. But when he had tasted it, he refused to drink. After they had crucified him, they divided his garments by casting lots; then they sat down and kept watch over him there. And they placed over his head the written charge against him: This is Jesus, the King of the Jews. Two revolutionaries were crucified with him, one on his right and the other on his left. Those passing by reviled him, shaking their heads and saying, "You who would destroy the temple and rebuild it in three days, save yourself, if you are the Son of God, and come down from the cross!" Likewise the chief priests with the scribes and elders mocked him and said, "He saved others;

he cannot save himself. So he is the king of Israel! Let him come down from the cross now, and we will believe in him. He trusted in God; let him deliver him now if he wants him. For he said, 'I am the Son of God.'" The revolutionaries who were crucified with him also kept abusing him in the same way.

From noon onward, darkness came over the whole land until three in the afternoon. And about three o'clock Jesus cried out in a loud voice, *"Eli, Eli, lema sabachthani?"* which means, "My God, my God, why have you forsaken me?" Some of the bystanders who heard it said, "This one is calling for Elijah." Immediately one of them ran to get a sponge; he soaked it in wine, and putting it on a reed, gave it to him to drink. But the rest said, "Wait, let us see if Elijah comes to save him." But Jesus cried out again in a loud voice, and gave up his spirit.

Here all kneel and pause for a short time.

And behold, the veil of the sanctuary was torn in two from top to bottom. The earth quaked, rocks were split, tombs were opened, and the bodies of many saints who had fallen asleep were raised. And coming forth from their tombs after his resurrection, they entered the holy city and appeared to many. The centurion and the men with him who were keeping watch over Jesus feared greatly when they saw the earthquake and all that was happening, and they said, "Truly, this was the Son of God!"

Brief Silence

For Reflection

The disciples are strong in their claim that they will stand by Jesus, but their actions hardly bear this out. They fall asleep—three times!—in the garden when Jesus asks them to watch and pray with him. They flee when Jesus is arrested. Peter not only denies knowing Jesus—three times!—but does so "with an oath" and with cursing and swearing. Standing by someone we love, having faith in that person, is easy when there is no cost. Jesus warns the disciples at the Last Supper that their faith would be shaken, but the disciples deny that this will ever happen. Nonetheless, faith is greatly threatened when there is great cost and we instinctively protect ourselves: the disciples flee; the Jewish leaders are adamant about destroying Jesus. Jesus alone remains unshaken in his faith: in the Garden he says yes to his Father's will, he is silent before his accusers' false accusations, he willingly gives up his spirit on the cross. Instead of protecting himself, Jesus embraces the cost of his suffering and death—the great sign of his own faithfulness. An even greater sign is yet to come.

✦ What helps me to remain faithful to my commitment to Jesus, even when facing great cost, is . . .

Brief Silence

Prayer

Lord, preserve us from ever fleeing from the cost of following faithfully in your Son's Gospel journey. But when we do stray and take the easy road, gently bring us back to your loving embrace and enkindle in us a fire of fervent fidelity. We ask this through Christ our Lord. **Amen**.

Remembering Jesus' great gift of himself in the Eucharist, we begin our prayer and reflection by examining how well we have loved others and given thanks for the Body and Blood of Christ . . .

Prayer

God our Father, your Son showed us the meaning of love by stooping to wash the feet of his disciples. Help us to reach out to others with the same self-giving love as Jesus, and to serve you faithfully by willingly serving others. We ask this through Christ our Lord. **Amen**.

Gospel (John 13:1-15)

Before the feast of Passover, Jesus knew that his hour had come to pass from this world to the Father. He loved his own in the world and he loved them to the end. The devil had already induced Judas, son of Simon the Iscariot, to hand him over. So, during supper, fully aware that the Father had put everything into his power and that he had come from God and was returning to God, he rose from supper and took off his outer garments. He took a towel and tied it around his waist. Then he poured water into a basin and began to wash the disciples' feet and dry them with the towel around his waist. He came to Simon Peter, who said to him, "Master, are you going to wash my feet?" Jesus answered and said to him, "What I am doing, you do not understand now, but you will understand later." Peter said to him, "You will never wash my feet." Jesus answered him, "Unless I wash you, you will have no inheritance with me." Simon Peter said to him, "Master, then not only my feet, but my hands and head as well." Jesus said to him, "Whoever has bathed has no need except to have his feet washed, for he is clean all over; so you are clean, but not all." For he knew who would betray him; for this reason, he said, "Not all of you are clean."

So when he had washed their feet and put his garments back on and reclined at table again, he said to them, "Do you realize what I have done for you? You call me 'teacher' and 'master,' and rightly so, for indeed I am. If I, therefore, the master and teacher, have washed your feet, you ought to wash one another's feet. I have given you a model to follow, so that as I have done for you, you should also do."

Brief Silence

For Reflection

The import of the self-giving footwashing is that we, Jesus' followers, "should also do." This is a symbolic act—in our society today we are hardly expected to take a basin and begin washing the feet of our dinner guests. What is expected of faithful followers of Jesus is to recognize in others the glory of God, to respect the dignity of all others, to be agents of fidelity and justice, to be inclusive in our relationships, to lift the burdens of others, to love without reserve and without expectations of reward or return. These actions modeled first by Jesus are carried out in the ordinary circumstances of our daily living. Being so risky as to smile and pleasantly greet a perfect stranger on the street who looks tired or agitated, being patient with the children who demand our attention, planning a special meal simply to surprise the family on an ordinary day are all ways we manifest God's glory. The possibilities are unlimited for us to do as Jesus did; all we need to do is follow the model he gave us. In being his Presence for others, we manifest God's glory. We share in God's holiness.

✦ Self-giving love is easiest for me when . . . It is most difficult for me when . . .

Brief Silence

Prayer

When we receive the Body and Blood of your Son, God our Father, we are nourished to live the Gospel message he taught us. May we grow in our love for the Eucharist and our love for each other. We ask this through Christ our Lord. **Amen**.

As we begin our time of prayer and reflection, we turn our hearts to our risen Lord to encounter him in his glorious, risen Life . . .

Prayer

God of Life, you raised your Son from death to the glory of risen Life. As we share in this same risen Life through the graciousness of your grace, may we be faithful to its promise and live its demands. We ask this through Christ our Lord. **Amen**.

Gospel (John 20:1-9)

On the first day of the week, Mary of Magdala came to the tomb early in the morning, while it was still dark, and saw the stone removed from the tomb. So she ran and went to Simon Peter and to the other disciple whom Jesus loved, and told them, "They have taken the Lord from the tomb, and we don't know where they put him." So Peter and the other disciple went out and came to the tomb. They both ran, but the other disciple ran faster than Peter and arrived at the tomb first; he bent down and saw the burial cloths there, but did not go in. When Simon Peter arrived after him, he went into the tomb and saw the burial cloths there, and the cloth that had covered his head, not with the burial cloths but rolled up in a separate place. Then the other disciple also went in, the one who had arrived at the tomb first, and he saw and believed. For they did not yet understand the Scripture that he had to rise from the dead.

Brief Silence

For Reflection

An empty home means empty hearts. A full home means happy hearts. An empty tomb means empty hearts—but no, it doesn't. Mary found an empty tomb and ran to find Peter and the beloved disciple and spoke from an empty heart; she thought the dead body had been stolen. They had not yet come to understanding. But the empty tomb also gave birth to hopeful hearts, hearts ready to believe even though they did not understand, hearts that would become filled with the glory of risen Life. Like the disciples in this account, we have no immediate evidence of Jesus' resurrection. Rather, that glorious event is mediated to us in the same way it was for those disciples long ago. For us, Jesus' risen Presence is mediated through witness-disciples who by their Gospel living announce that Jesus is alive and with us, who announce Jesus' glorious, risen Presence by the way they live. The mystery is beyond us at the same time it is within us! The Lord is truly risen! What a glorious morn to which this darkness gives way! What emptiness glory fills!

✦ I am overjoyed to bring the glorious, risen Presence of Christ to others in these ways . . .

Brief Silence

Prayer

Glorious God of Life, you fill our hearts with joy as we celebrate the resurrection of Jesus Christ. May our joy overflow into good works that announce to others the risen Presence within and among us. We ask this through Christ our Lord. **Amen.**

Through our baptism we receive the Holy Spirit, the Presence of the risen Lord within and among us. Let us ask God to be with us during our prayer and reflection and to be more attentive to the Spirit within . . .

Prayer

Gift-giving God, your Holy Spirit is within and among us. As we celebrate the risen Presence of Christ during this Easter season, may we come to deeper belief in your abiding Presence. We ask this through Christ our Lord. **Amen**.

Gospel (John 20:19-31)

On the evening of that first day of the week, when the doors were locked, where the disciples were, for fear of the Jews, Jesus came and stood in their midst and said to them, "Peace be with you." When he had said this, he showed them his hands and his side. The disciples rejoiced when they saw the Lord. Jesus said to them again, "Peace be with you. As the Father has sent me, so I send you." And when he had said this, he breathed on them and said to them, "Receive the Holy Spirit. Whose sins you forgive are forgiven them, and whose sins you retain are retained."

Thomas, called Didymus, one of the Twelve, was not with them when Jesus came. So the other disciples said to him, "We have seen the Lord." But he said to them, "Unless I see the mark of the nails in his hands and put my finger into the nailmarks and put my hand into his side, I will not believe."

Now a week later his disciples were again inside and Thomas was with them. Jesus came, although the doors were locked, and stood in their midst and said, "Peace be with you." Then he said to Thomas, "Put your finger here and see my hands, and bring your hand and put it into my side, and do not be unbelieving, but believe." Thomas answered and said to him, "My Lord and my God!"

Jesus said to him, "Have you come to believe because you have seen me? Blessed are those who have not seen and have believed."

Now, Jesus did many other signs in the presence of his disciples that are not written in this book. But these are written that you may come to believe that Jesus is the Christ, the Son of God, and that through this belief you may have life in his name.

Brief Silence

For Reflection

The basic issue in this gospel story is coming to believe that Jesus is risen and alive. What is made clear is that believing is not dependent on physical contact with Jesus (Thomas makes his profession of faith without touching Jesus), but coming to believe does depend on personal encounter. Authentic encounter between persons only happens through mutual self-giving: Jesus' self-giving is shown through his gift of the Holy Spirit to us; our self-giving is shown when we open ourselves to receive that Spirit. What a Gift!

Jesus' Spirit enables the personal encounter between us and the risen Lord; the Spirit enables us to come to believe without touching, but by giving ourselves over to *receiving*. With mutual self-giving new, risen Life is experienced. With mutual self-giving we do not need tangible proof that Jesus is alive. But we do need the giving and receiving of the Spirit. Believing, moreover, is actually made tangible in the mutual self-giving of authentic encounter between Person and person. In turn, this empowers us to experience the mutual self-giving of authentic encounter between us and others. Such a Gift Jesus breathes upon us! Such a Gift we exchange with others!

✦ The manner of my giving Holy Communion to others deepens their belief in the risen Lord whenever I . . .

Brief Silence

Prayer

Glorious God of the resurrection, your Son comes to us under the signs of bread and wine. As we receive the Body and Blood of the risen Christ, may we grow in our openness to encounter you in those we meet every day as we strive to be self-giving as the risen Christ. We ask this through Christ our Lord. **Amen**.

Through Scripture and the breaking of the bread Jesus revealed his risen Presence to the disciples on the road to Emmaus. Let us open our hearts to this same Presence to us now during our prayer and reflection . . .

Prayer

God of the resurrection, your Son is ever present to us on our own journey of life as we share in Word and sacrament. May that Word burn in our hearts and move us to care for others; may that sacrament fill us with the joy of risen Life. We ask this through Christ our Lord. **Amen.**

Gospel (Luke 24:13-35)

That very day, the first day of the week, two of Jesus' disciples were going to a village seven miles from Jerusalem called Emmaus, and they were conversing about all the things that had occurred. And it happened that while they were conversing and debating, Jesus himself drew near and walked with them, but their eyes were prevented from recognizing him. He asked them, "What are you discussing as you walk along?" They stopped, looking downcast. One of them, named Cleopas, said to him in reply, "Are you the only visitor to Jerusalem who does not know of the things that have taken place there in these days?" And he replied to them, "What sort of things?" They said to him, "The things that happened to Jesus the Nazarene, who was a prophet mighty in deed and word before God and all the people, how our chief priests and rulers both handed him over to a sentence of death and crucified him. But we were hoping that he would be the one to redeem Israel; and besides all this, it is now the third day since this took place. Some women from our group, however, have astounded us: they were at the tomb early in the morning and did not find his body; they came back and reported that they had indeed seen a vision of angels who announced that he was alive. Then some of those with us went to the tomb and found things just as the women had described, but him they did not see." And he said to them, "Oh, how foolish you are! How slow of heart to believe all that the prophets spoke! Was it not necessary that the Christ should suffer these things and enter into his glory?" Then beginning with Moses and all the prophets, he interpreted to them what referred to him in all the Scriptures. As they approached the village to which they were going, he gave the impression that he was going on farther. But they urged him, "Stay with us, for it is nearly evening and the day is almost over." So he went in to stay with them. And it happened that, while he was with them at table, he took bread, said the blessing, broke it, and gave it to them. With that their eyes were opened and they recognized him, but he vanished from their sight. Then they said to each other, "Were not our hearts burning within us while he spoke to us on the way and opened the Scriptures to us?" So they set out at once and returned to Jerusalem where they found gathered together the eleven and those with them who were saying, "The Lord has truly been raised and has appeared to Simon!" Then the two recounted what had taken place on the way and how he was made known to them in the breaking of the bread.

Brief Silence

For Reflection

On our own we cannot grasp the mystery of the resurrection, of Easter Life. The two disciples on the road to Emmaus were "conversing and debating"; they could recount the facts of "all the things that had occurred" in Jerusalem on the previous days, but could not believe the mystery. Yet they greatly desired to move from disappointment and unbelief to hearts burning with life and belief—they invited Jesus to stay the night with them. Jesus had piqued their desire to delve deeper into the mystery; they wanted to hear more. Their engagement through Jesus with the living word of Scripture and their recognition of the risen Jesus in the breaking of the bread brought these two disciples to believe beyond the facts to the reality that Jesus is alive.

Our own participation in Word and sacrament must give rise to the same desire in us: to seek Life by journeying deeper into the mystery. Word and sacrament must move us to delve deeper into the mystery of the risen Life that Jesus continually offers us. The two disciples did not want to believe the facts of the Jerusalem events that first Good Friday, Holy Saturday, and Easter Sunday. That is, until they knew *all* the facts. Coming to recognize Jesus, coming to believe that he had risen, unveiled more facts for them. But the mystery still wasn't finished. These disciples and all of us who choose to follow Jesus spend our whole lives journeying with Jesus, learning more "facts" about this risen Life he so generously offers us. Our participation in Word and sacrament is our walk with Jesus through life during which he continues to teach us that he is risen and present.

✦ The Communion procession moves me along my Emmaus journey when . . .

Brief Silence

Prayer

Wondrous God, you come to us in most unexpected ways in the everyday events of our simple lives. Be with us as we strive to live the mystery of risen Life more faithfully and come to an ever deeper appreciation for the gift of your divine Son. We ask this through Christ our Lord. **Amen.**

We ask God to bless us during our prayer and reflection. Let us prepare ourselves to hear Jesus' voice and follow his call . . .

Prayer

God of abundant Life, you invite us into your divine Presence by entering through the wide-open gate of your Son's open heart. Help us to recognize his voice calling us and to follow his way of goodness and love. We ask this through Christ our Lord. **Amen**.

Gospel (John 10:1-10)

Jesus said: "Amen, amen, I say to you, whoever does not enter a sheepfold through the gate but climbs over elsewhere is a thief and a robber. But whoever enters through the gate is the shepherd of the sheep. The gatekeeper opens it for him, and the sheep hear his voice, as the shepherd calls his own sheep by name and leads them out. When he has driven out all his own, he walks ahead of them, and the sheep follow him, because they recognize his voice. But they will not follow a stranger; they will run away from him, because they do not recognize the voice of strangers." Although Jesus used this figure of speech, the Pharisees did not realize what he was trying to tell them.

So Jesus said again, "Amen, amen, I say to you, I am the gate for the sheep. All who came before me are thieves and robbers, but the sheep did not listen to them. I am the gate. Whoever enters through me will be saved, and will come in and go out and find pasture. A thief comes only to steal and slaughter and destroy; I came so that they might have life and have it more abundantly."

Brief Silence

For Reflection

The wide-open gate is the goodness of the Shepherd. The twist of the gospel is that the gate is also a symbol for the Shepherd and how the Shepherd acts toward us—the gate itself is a metaphor for Jesus' care, his openness to call and welcome everyone, his desire to protect and guard us. Thus, the gate (the Good Shepherd) invites us to cross through, to enter into the safety and protection Jesus offers. The gate opens up a space of security, peace, and protection ("Whoever enters through me will be saved"). This is where resurrection faith calls us to enter the Gate, "that [we] might have life and have it more abundantly." Jesus states clearly that he came so that his followers might have abundant Life. Jesus uses the metaphor of a caring shepherd and sheep to indicate how his followers might receive that Life: by hearing his voice and their name, by following the Good Shepherd, by recognizing whose voice calls them. Hearing, following, recognizing: we are to open our ears in faith, open our hearts in trust, open our minds in love. This is the way to abundant Life. The Gate is wide open. Will we enter?

✦ My "Body [Blood] of Christ" is the voice of the Good Shepherd calling communicants to abundant Life when I . . .

Brief Silence

Prayer

O Shepherd God, you care for us with a tenderness beyond our imagining and protect us from any harm. Strengthen us through Holy Communion to remain faithfully in the risen Lord's sheepfold and never to stray from his love. We ask this through Christ our Lord. **Amen**.

Jesus is our way, truth, and life. He is our all. As we prepare to encounter him during our prayer and reflection, may we open our hearts to his risen Presence and surrender to him to lead us to his Father.

Prayer

You graciously offer us risen Life, gracious God, as we strive to follow in the narrow way of truth and life that Jesus taught us. Reassure us with your love, ease our troubled hearts when we are not as faithful as we wish to be, and bring us to the fullness of risen Life. We ask this through Christ our Lord. **Amen**.

Gospel (John 14:1-12)

Jesus said to his disciples: "Do not let your hearts be troubled. You have faith in God; have faith also in me. In my Father's house there are many dwelling places. If there were not, would I have told you that I am going to prepare a place for you? And if I go and prepare a place for you, I will come back again and take you to myself, so that where I am you also may be. Where I am going you know the way." Thomas said to him, "Master, we do not know where you are going; how can we know the way?" Jesus said to him, "I am the way and the truth and the life. No one comes to the Father except through me. If you know me, then you will also know my Father. From now on you do know him and have seen him." Philip said to him, "Master, show us the Father, and that will be enough for us." Jesus said to him, "Have I been with you for so long a time and you still do not know me, Philip? Whoever has seen me has seen the Father. How can you say, 'Show us the Father'? Do you not believe that I am in the Father and the Father is in me? The words that I speak to you I do not speak on my own.

The Father who dwells in me is doing his works. Believe me that I am in the Father and the Father is in me, or else, believe because of the works themselves. Amen, amen, I say to you, whoever believes in me will do the works that I do, and will do greater ones than these, because I am going to the Father."

Brief Silence

For Reflection

Jesus' words in this gospel from the Last Supper discourse are reassuring ones: "Do not let your hearts be troubled." Yet Thomas and Philip, who hear Jesus also tell them that he is leaving, are not reassured and question him anxiously. The leap from the Jesus at the Last Supper to the Jesus after the resurrection is one giant step, one the disciples have not yet taken. These disciples cannot at this point understand that Jesus' leave-taking is not permanent; he is not abandoning his disciples. They have not come to understand what it means for Jesus to rise from the dead. But *we* have taken this leap. We are an Easter people. We have received the Holy Spirit who empowers us to know Jesus, through him to know the Father, and to do the works of Jesus. Believing this mitigates all troubles, all anxiety. Believing this helps us know the way to Jesus and to the Father. The gospel is challenging us to enter into a profound relationship with the risen Jesus, which ultimately means we share a profound relationship with the Father as well, through their Spirit of love.

✦ My Easter faith touches those to whom I bring Holy Communion and leads them to . . .

Brief Silence

Prayer

Our hearts are grateful, gracious God, for the gift of the Holy Spirit who leads us and guides us in right ways. May our communion with your risen Son strengthen our hope in one day receiving the fullness of his risen Life. We ask this through Christ our Lord. **Amen**.

God pours divine love into our hearts through the Spirit and calls us to newness of Life in Christ. Let us celebrate God's love and Life as we open ourselves to the divine Presence during our prayer and reflection . . .

Prayer

God of love, help us to change the "if" of love to a sure turning toward you that is witnessed by our willingness to obey your commandments. Help us to deepen our love for you and one another so that our relationships might grow and bear fruit. We ask this through Christ our Lord. **Amen**.

Gospel (John 14:15-21)

Jesus said to his disciples: "If you love me, you will keep my commandments. And I will ask the Father, and he will give you another Advocate to be with you always, the Spirit of truth, whom the world cannot accept, because it neither sees nor knows him. But you know him, because he remains with you, and will be in you. I will not leave you orphans; I will come to you. In a little while the world will no longer see me, but you will see me, because I live and you will live. On that day you will realize that I am in my Father and you are in me and I in you. Whoever has my commandments and observes them is the one who loves me. And whoever loves me will be loved by my Father, and I will love him and reveal myself to him."

Brief Silence

For Reflection

The gospel this Sunday shows us another way to look at commandments—as expressions of our love for God. Keeping commandments must always be within the context of love. Commandments cannot be isolated laws kept for their own sake; if so, this only tends to breed resentment and anger and fear. Jesus suggests that we keep his commandments because our love for him has established a deep and intimate relationship between us that spills out into acts we know will be pleasing to the Beloved. Thus, love is revealed in a threefold action: Jesus loves his disciples by revealing himself to them; the Father shows love by sending the Spirit to dwell with disciples always; disciples love Jesus by keeping his commandments. The fruit of all this loving is intimate relationship with Jesus and the Father, and faithfulness in keeping commandments. Thus, Jesus assures us we are not alone, we are not orphans. We are the beloved of God. In order to love Jesus, we must "see" the Spirit. This is only possible if we, through the goodness of our daily living, continue to deepen the love relationship we have with God. Love makes all things visible.

✦ Jesus is made visible in me and the communicants when . . .

Brief Silence

Prayer

God of love, you desire that we give ourselves over to your goodness and gifts. Help us to grow in our love for you and each other so that we might be a faithful Presence, through the Holy Spirit, of your abiding love. We ask this through Christ our Lord. **Amen**.

We celebrate Jesus' ascension to the heavens and commissioning of his disciples to continue his saving mission. Let us ask God during our prayer to help us be faithful disciples . . .

Prayer

Ageless God, you never withdraw your Presence from us and always strengthen us to respond to your divine Son's command to continue his saving mission. May we always be faithful to that mission, furthering your reign here on earth. We ask this through Christ our Lord. **Amen**.

Gospel (Matt 28:16-20)

The eleven disciples went to Galilee, to the mountain to which Jesus had ordered them. When they saw him, they worshiped, but they doubted. Then Jesus approached and said to them, "All power in heaven and on earth has been given to me. Go, therefore, and make disciples of all nations, baptizing them in the name of the Father, and of the Son, and of the Holy Spirit, teaching them to observe all that I have commanded you. And behold, I am with you always, until the end of the age."

Brief Silence

For Reflection

The continuation of Jesus' saving mission is so serious that Jesus issues the most serious and unequivocal of directives. The disciples are to begin where Jesus did, doing what Jesus did, but without geographical or temporal limits: their mission is to "all nations" and continues "until the end of the age." In effect, then, Jesus commissions not only those first disciples, but all those through the ages who come to know and believe in him. Jesus chooses to complete his work of salvation through us. We must choose to take up his Great Commission. Jesus' ascension into heaven is not a reward for what he did on earth, nor a ticket out of this world! Jesus' ascension is a return to his rightful place at the right hand of the Father. Yet Jesus did not absent himself after his ascension, but becomes present to us in a new way. This new Presence of Jesus is, through the power of the Spirit, *within us* ("I am with you always, until the end of the age") and is manifested when we continue Jesus' saving work as his disciples.

✦ I help those coming to receive Holy Communion grasp better that Jesus is always with us when . . .

Brief Silence

Prayer
Such divine Life you give us, O holy God, to strengthen us to continue Jesus' saving mission. Nourish us on Word and sacrament so that we might be faithful to his commands and receive the promise of fullness of Life with you forever. We ask this through Christ our Lord. **Amen**.

Jesus' dying and rising opens for us a share in the very Life and holiness of God. Let us open ourselves to God's transforming action as we encounter the divine Presence and holiness during our prayer . . .

Prayer

God of Life and glory, fill us with your Presence and goodness through the Holy Spirit. May peace reign in our hearts and spread to all those we encounter in our everyday lives. We ask this through Christ our Lord. **Amen**.

Gospel (John 17:1-11a)

Jesus raised his eyes to heaven and said, "Father, the hour has come. Give glory to your son, so that your son may glorify you, just as you gave him authority over all people, so that your son may give eternal life to all you gave him. Now this is eternal life, that they should know you, the only true God, and the one whom you sent, Jesus Christ. I glorified you on earth by accomplishing the work that you gave me to do. Now glorify me, Father, with you, with the glory that I had with you before the world began.

"I revealed your name to those whom you gave me out of the world. They belonged to you, and you gave them to me, and they have kept your word. Now they know that everything you gave me is from you, because the words you gave to me I have given to them, and they accepted them and truly understood that I came from you, and they have believed that you sent me. I pray for them. I do not pray for the world but for the ones you have given me, because they are yours, and everything of mine is yours and everything of yours is mine, and I have been glorified in them. And now I will no longer be in the world, but they are in the world, while I am coming to you."

Brief Silence

For Reflection

In this gospel Jesus speaks of his and his Father's glory—but his words are not a reminiscing at the Last Supper of what has been but will soon be no more. No, this glory of which Jesus speaks is an eternal glory. Glory is the tangible trace in our world of God's holiness—who God is. Jesus' prayer is about his union with his Father, and it also expresses his desire for us to share in this same union, same glory, same holiness. Nothing of Jesus is withheld from us—he yearns to give us eternal Life. Indeed, God's Life within us is already glorification. We normally think of our share in Jesus' glory as a future event which will happen after our natural death. But by the gift and Presence of the Spirit in us, we already share in God's Life. Yes, glorification is taking place even now! The Scripture message is so simple and clear: God is glorified when we take up Jesus' work. And in this we already share in Jesus' glory. Nevertheless, this assurance and promise of sharing in Jesus' glory ought not to cloud our vision—a share in glory first entails a share in the self-giving sacrifice of Jesus as well.

✦ The acclamation "Body (Blood) of Christ" includes the reality of sharing "in the sufferings of Christ" in that . . .

Brief Silence

Prayer

Eternal God, your glory shines forth in your risen Son. May that same glory shine forth in us as we strive to be faithful to all you ask of us. We ask this through Christ our Lord. **Amen**.

Pentecost celebrates the coming of the Spirit who empowers us to take up Christ's saving mission. Let us ask God to be faithful to this Spirit who dwells within us . . .

Prayer

Come, O Holy Spirit, and empower us to live the Gospel with courage and fidelity. May we bask in the peace you bring as we spread Jesus' message of forgiveness and healing to all we meet in our daily living. We ask this through Christ our Lord. **Amen**.

Gospel (John 20:19-23)

On the evening of that first day of the week, when the doors were locked, where the disciples were, for fear of the Jews, Jesus came and stood in their midst and said to them, "Peace be with you." When he had said this, he showed them his hands and his side. The disciples rejoiced when they saw the Lord. Jesus said to them again, "Peace be with you. As the Father has sent me, so I send you." And when he had said this, he breathed on them and said to them, "Receive the Holy Spirit. Whose sins you forgive are forgiven them, and whose sins you retain are retained."

Brief Silence

For Reflection

One of the fruits of the Holy Spirit is peace. This peace is not a passive state of tranquility, but an empowering force which allays our fears, urges us forth to take up Jesus' mission, and instills in us forgiving hearts. This peace transforms how we see ourselves, how we pursue discipleship, and how we relate to the world and one another. Certainly, this peace is life-encompassing and enduring. How much more so is Jesus' gift of the Holy Spirit!

The Spirit unleashes a twofold energy within us: the Spirit draws us *into* Christ and sends us *out* to proclaim Christ to the world. Jesus *breathes* on the disciples and ushers in a new creation, enabling the disciples to take up Jesus' work. Clearly, the gift of the Spirit is for the sake of Jesus' mission: "so I send you . . . Receive the Holy Spirit." Pentecost—the coming of the Spirit—happens each time we do the works of God and manifest the Spirit for the benefit of all. Through the indwelling of the Spirit we are able to carry on Jesus' saving mission, for the Spirit re-creates us in Jesus' image and empowers us to live the Gospel faithfully.

✦ I experience the power of the Holy Spirit transforming me to . . .

Brief Silence

Prayer

O divine Breath of God, imbue us with peace, patience, joy, kindness, strength. As we continue Jesus' saving mission, help us never to forget that you dwell within us, keep us faithful, and bring us to the fullness of risen Life. We ask this through Christ our Lord. **Amen**.

Let us pause in silence
to open our hearts to the
Presence of our triune God,
remembering that God is
always with us . . .

Prayer

Triune God, the mystery of your unity is sure, the diversity of your divine Persons beckons us to reach out to the immense diversity of persons around us. Help us to welcome everyone into our care and love them with the love that you shower on us. We ask this through Christ our Lord. **Amen**.

Gospel (John 3:16-18)

God so loved the world that he gave his only Son, so that everyone who believes in him might not perish but might have eternal life. For God did not send his Son into the world to condemn the world, but that the world might be saved through him. Whoever believes in him will not be condemned, but whoever does not believe has already been condemned, because he has not believed in the name of the only Son of God.

Brief Silence

For Reflection

God came down in a cloud on Mount Sinai, drawing near to Moses and revealing the divine Self to him as merciful, gracious, kind, and faithful. Yet even this wonderful divine self-revelation was exceeded when God "gave his only Son" so that we might be saved. But even more: the fullest revelation of the grace, love, and fellowship of the Trinity is extended to us believers with the sending of the Spirit as a share in divine intimacy—eternal Life itself. God chooses to be very near to us. God's desire is that we share in divine Life eternally. To this end, God is very near—near to Moses on Mount Sinai and near to us in the divine Son who came to dwell among us. Even more: for those who believe, our triune God dwells *within* us by grace and communion, drawing us into the inner Life of the Trinity. The unceasing Life of the Trinity is this: to love us into eternal Life. It is God's gracious gift, and ours to choose. In this is eternal Life: to be absorbed into the very Persons of God.

✦ The manner with which I embrace my ministry is a witness to my choosing to believe in God's nearness in that . . .

Brief Silence

Prayer

O God, you draw near to us and offer us the gift of your triune Life. May we open ourselves to your divine Presence, allow you to transform us into your graciousness, and live the Gospel with the resolve to witness to your love and care. We ask this through Christ our Lord. **Amen**.

Jesus gives us a great gift in the Eucharist—his very self as our food and drink. Let us pause and reflect on how we have been nourished by this gift and strengthened for our own self-giving . . .

Prayer

O ever-living God, your divine Son gives himself to us as living bread that nourishes us for our salvation. Raise us up with new courage to live the eucharistic mystery of self-giving, to be faithful to our identity as the Body of Christ to be given for others, and to witness to the Gospel in all the events of our daily living. We ask this through Christ our Lord. **Amen.**

Gospel (John 6:51-58)

Jesus said to the Jewish crowds: "I am the living bread that came down from heaven; whoever eats this bread will live forever; and the bread that I will give is my flesh for the life of the world."

The Jews quarreled among themselves, saying, "How can this man give us his flesh to eat?" Jesus said to them, "Amen, amen, I say to you, unless you eat the flesh of the Son of Man and drink his blood, you do not have life within you. Whoever eats my flesh and drinks my blood has eternal life, and I will raise him on the last day. For my flesh is true food, and my blood is true drink. Whoever eats my flesh and drinks my blood remains in me and I in him. Just as the living Father sent me and I have life because of the Father, so also the one who feeds on me will have life because of me. This is the bread that came down from heaven. Unlike your ancestors who ate and still died, whoever eats this bread will live forever."

Brief Silence

For Reflection

In this gospel Jesus asserts twice (at the beginning and again at the end) that "whoever eats this bread will live forever." This forever is not a measurable forever and cannot be grasped by passing time. This forever is Life in communion with Jesus that never ends. This gospel presents in a most astonishing way how we participate in Jesus' forever, in eternal Life. It also presents in a most astonishing way the very core of the mystery we celebrate on this solemnity—the mystery of Jesus' giving us his flesh and blood as our eternal food and drink. Jesus' declaration that he is the "bread that came down from heaven" grounds his further declaration that those who eat "this bread will live forever." Heaven is a state of forever; those who eat the One come down from heaven will be like he is—in a state of forever. This lofty promise is no pie in the sky dreaming. It is real because Jesus himself has passed from this life to eternal glory. His humanity has risen and now lives forever. It is this risen humanity which is our nourishment for eternal Life.

✦ My ministry is truly eucharistic (that is, an act of self-giving in love) when I . . .

Brief Silence

Prayer

God of mystery, the Eucharist is a gift beyond compare and the promise of the fullness of Life. May our hearts brim with gratitude for this great Gift, may we approach the table of your banquet with reverence and awe, and may we strive to be self-giving like Jesus. We ask this through Christ our Lord. **Amen**.

Saints Peter and Paul were rocks upon which Jesus built his church because they knew who Jesus was and remained faithful to the mission he gave them. Let us open our hearts during our prayer to come to know Jesus more fully and follow him more faithfully . . .

Prayer

Good God, you give us Saints Peter and Paul as models of holiness and strength. As they were faithful to Jesus and his saving mission, so may we imitate their lives and holiness. We ask this through Christ our Lord. **Amen**.

Gospel (Matt 16:13-19)

When Jesus went into the region of Caesarea Philippi he asked his disciples, "Who do people say that the Son of Man is?" They replied, "Some say John the Baptist, others Elijah, still others Jeremiah or one of the prophets." He said to them, "But who do you say that I am?" Simon Peter said in reply, "You are the Christ, the Son of the living God." Jesus said to him in reply, "Blessed are you, Simon son of Jonah. For flesh and blood has not revealed this to you, but my heavenly Father. And so I say to you, you are Peter, and upon this rock I will build my Church, and the gates of the netherworld shall not prevail against it. I will give you the keys to the Kingdom of heaven. Whatever you bind on earth shall be bound in heaven; and whatever you loose on earth shall be loosed in heaven."

Brief Silence

For Reflection

"Who am I?" This question Jesus put to his disciples long ago remains a question for all times and all disciples. To be faithful rocks upon which the church is built, we must know who Jesus is for us, listen to what he teaches us, and guard against anything prevailing against his church. Peter and Paul's faithful and fruitful discipleship rested on the rock of their knowing Jesus. Our own faithful and fruitful discipleship rests on this same rock. Drawing from our everyday experience of rocks, we must be unyielding when it comes to living what Jesus has taught us, rock solid when it comes to following him, rock steady in our commitment to bring his love and care to others.

This solemnity celebrates two rocks of our faith. But this solemnity celebrates more than two great apostles. Peter and Paul represent all believers who come to faith and acknowledge who Christ is, and who keep the faith by fulfilling their part in the mission of Jesus. This solemnity celebrates the establishment of the church. Most of all, this solemnity celebrates the victory of Christ that is shared with his faithful disciples—the fullness of Life forever.

✦ Over the years my answers to Jesus' question "Who do you say that I am?" have been . . .

Brief Silence

Prayer

Holy God, Saints Peter and Paul enjoy the fullness of Life, standing ever before the throne of your divine Majesty offering unending praise. May our own praise be constant, our gratitude full, and our seeking your divine Presence diligent. We ask this through Christ our Lord. **Amen**.

Jesus invites us to come to him. Let us ready our hearts once again to encounter Jesus who is meek and humble of heart . . .

Prayer

God of love, your Son invites us to yoke ourselves to him who makes our burdens light. May we find rest in him and be humbled by his care for us. We ask this through Christ our Lord. **Amen**.

Gospel (Matt 11:25-30)

At that time Jesus exclaimed: "I give praise to you, Father, Lord of heaven and earth, for although you have hidden these things from the wise and the learned you have revealed them to little ones. Yes, Father, such has been your gracious will. All things have been handed over to me by my Father. No one knows the Son except the Father, and no one knows the Father except the Son and anyone to whom the Son wishes to reveal him.

"Come to me, all you who labor and are burdened, and I will give you rest. Take my yoke upon you and learn from me, for I am meek and humble of heart; and you will find rest for yourselves. For my yoke is easy, and my burden light."

Brief Silence

For Reflection

In this gospel Jesus is the messianic Savior judging those who are unfaithful or faithful. The faithful, having come to Jesus and taken his yoke upon themselves, live in God's peace now. These faithful ones need have no fear of Jesus' judgment. Scattered throughout this gospel passage are a number of contrasts that present us with the choice to be faithful or not: hidden // revealed; wise and learned // little ones; no one knows // reveals the Father; labor and are burdened // rest; unknowing // learn from Jesus; yoke // easy and light burden. The first term of each pair points to those who are unfaithful, those who cannot hear Jesus' message of Good News calling them to repentance, those who call upon themselves a judgment of death. The second term of each pair points to those who are faithful, those who hear Jesus' message and change their lives, those who receive a judgment of life. The rest Jesus offers, the easy and light burden, is possible for the faithful because they need not fear Jesus' judgment. Jesus gives us shelter from every storm. He warns us of every destructive enemy. He yokes us to himself and assures us of Life and peace.

✦ Receiving Holy Communion yokes me to Christ and others in these ways . . .

Brief Silence

Prayer

God of peace and comfort, we rest ourselves in you. As we unite ourselves to you and the risen Son, may our burdens be light and our praise be constant as we look forward to fullness of Life forever. We ask this through Christ our Lord. **Amen**.

God's word comes to us in many ways to bear fruit in our lives. Let us prepare our hearts to hear God's word during our prayer and reflection . . .

Prayer

O God, you speak your divine word and life bursts forth. May we hear your word with greater fervor, let it enter deeply into our hearts, and live it with exuberance and joy. We ask this through Christ our Lord. **Amen**.

Gospel (Matt 13:1-9 [Longer Form: Matt 13:1-23])

On that day, Jesus went out of the house and sat down by the sea. Such large crowds gathered around him that he got into a boat and sat down, and the whole crowd stood along the shore. And he spoke to them at length in parables, saying: "A sower went out to sow. And as he sowed, some seed fell on the path, and birds came and ate it up. Some fell on rocky ground, where it had little soil. It sprang up at once because the soil was not deep, and when the sun rose it was scorched, and it withered for lack of roots. Some seed fell among thorns, and the thorns grew up and choked it. But some seed fell on rich soil and produced fruit, a hundred or sixty or thirtyfold. Whoever has ears ought to hear."

Brief Silence

For Reflection

When we are trying to explain something important to another, we choose our words carefully, speak directly and clearly, and pause often to make sure our hearer is tracking with us. Jesus always speaks something important: he is opening our eyes

and ears to see and hear the growth and Life he offers us. But
sometimes it seems as though he does not speak very directly or
clearly. He speaks of the mystery of God's kingdom, of coming to
salvation, in parables, and leaves us multiple layers of rich seeds
to nurture and bring to fruitfulness. Both in the parable itself and
in Jesus' explanation of it, he indicates that seeds falling on rich
soil do not all produce the same abundance—some thirty, some
sixty, some a hundredfold. God cares less about quantity produced
and more about growth and life coming to fruition. As we take in
God's word with understanding hearts and come to conversion
and receive healing, God actually gives us more than even a hundredfold. God gives us fullness of Life forever.

✦ The new growth I experience from hearing God's word is
. . .

Brief Silence

Prayer

God of life, you send your divine Word to be with us and to teach
us how to live fruitful lives. May we be rich soil in which the seed
of your word takes root and produces a hundredfold of good
works that bring us to the fullness of Life everlasting. We ask this
through Christ our Lord. **Amen**.

God's Presence and reign is visible in our lives when we open ourselves to God's will for us. Let us pray that we might discern God's will for us more faithfully . . .

Prayer

Patient God, how good you are to us! You are patient while we discern how to serve you faithfully, patient when the weeds of our lives lead us to stray from you. Help us to grow strong in living the Gospel and may our lives reflect the coming of your reign. We ask this through Christ our Lord. **Amen**.

Gospel (Matt 13:24-30 [Longer Form: Matt 13:24-43])

Jesus proposed another parable to the crowds, saying: "The kingdom of heaven may be likened to a man who sowed good seed in his field. While everyone was asleep his enemy came and sowed weeds all through the wheat, and then went off. When the crop grew and bore fruit, the weeds appeared as well. The slaves of the householder came to him and said, 'Master, did you not sow good seed in your field? Where have the weeds come from?' He answered, 'An enemy has done this.' His slaves said to him, 'Do you want us to go and pull them up?' He replied, 'No, if you pull up the weeds you might uproot the wheat along with them. Let them grow together until harvest; then at harvest time I will say to the harvesters, "First collect the weeds and tie them in bundles for burning; but gather the wheat into my barn."'"

Brief Silence

For Reflection

"The kingdom of heaven is like . . ." Jesus uses three comparisons (in the longer form of the gospel) to explain this mystery of God's Presence and reign. The first parable speaks of discernment; the Master judged that to pull the weeds too soon could sacrifice the crop. Rather, he says, let "them grow together" and in the end it will be clear what to keep and what to throw out. Discernment always involves care, distinction, and judgment. The second parable speaks of full growth; with patience and care the tiny seed can grow into a full-grown, large bush that offers protection and dwelling for others of God's creatures. Full growth always involves becoming more than we are for the good of others. The third parable speaks of transformation; just a little yeast gives life, softness, and readiness to the dough. Transformation always involves new energy toward life, rising to new possibilities, being fashioned into someone new and surprising. In this is the realization of the kingdom of heaven: our discerning God's will, our growing into full stature as "children of the kingdom," opening ourselves to being transformed into those remaining faithful until "the end of the age."

✦ Some of the ways I nurture communicants so that the kingdom of heaven becomes visible for them is . . .

Brief Silence

Prayer

O God, you invite us to live in your kingdom now and in the age to come. Help us to remain faithful to your ways, to discern your will for us, and to be transformed into ever more perfect members of the Body of Christ. We ask this through Christ our Lord. **Amen**.

We pause to reflect on the great gift God has given us in Christ. He is our great treasure, our pearl of great price. Let us open ourselves to encounter him during our prayer . . .

Prayer

O God, generous giver of good gifts, you offer us the great treasure of living under your reign. May we hold the kingdom of heaven as the greatest treasure we possess and seek to live as faithful servants of your will. We ask this through Christ our Lord. **Amen**.

Gospel (Matt 13:44-52 or Matt 13:44-46)

Jesus said to his disciples: "The kingdom of heaven is like a treasure buried in a field, which a person finds and hides again, and out of joy goes and sells all that he has and buys that field. Again, the kingdom of heaven is like a merchant searching for fine pearls. When he finds a pearl of great price, he goes and sells all that he has and buys it. Again, the kingdom of heaven is like a net thrown into the sea, which collects fish of every kind. When it is full they haul it ashore and sit down to put what is good into buckets. What is bad they throw away. Thus it will be at the end of the age. The angels will go out and separate the wicked from the righteous and throw them into the fiery furnace, where there will be wailing and grinding of teeth.

"Do you understand all these things?" They answered, "Yes." And he replied, "Then every scribe who has been instructed in the kingdom of heaven is like the head of a household who brings from his storeroom both the new and the old."

Brief Silence

For Reflection

"The kingdom of heaven is like . . . " In these three parables, what motivates the actions of the person, merchant, and fishermen is that they have already come upon the extreme good which they seek: the treasure in the field, the pearl of great price, the catch of fish. They have encountered the treasure they desire; now they do what they must to have it. So it is with us. We have already come upon the extreme good which we spend our lives seeking: the kingdom of heaven. The challenge is to give our all to attain it. Nothing else we have is comparable to what God offers: a share in the kingdom of heaven. This kingdom of heaven must so grab us that nothing else in our life matters and everything we choose and do is motivated by opening ourselves to the gift of God's Presence. We must seek the wisdom to recognize the surpassing worth of the kingdom when it appears and be bold enough to stake all we have and are and do on the kingdom ("sells all"). The gospel thus invites us to be wise and to be bold! We must be active in seeking the fullness of God's kingdom.

✦ What motivates me to give all to attain the kingdom of heaven is . . .

Brief Silence

Prayer

Ever living and loving God, you desire that we share in the fullness of Life that you offer us. Be with us as we search for the great treasure you offer us in the many choices that face us each day, always remaining faithful to your divine will. We ask this through Christ our Lord. **Amen.**

Jesus feeds the five thousand with just five loaves and two fish. Let us open ourselves during our prayer and reflection to appreciate more deeply the bread from heaven Jesus gives us . . .

Prayer

Gracious God, you bless us and enable us to fill the needs of those who cross the paths of our lives. Help us to recognize your blessings and gifts to us and to give all we are for the good of others. We ask this through Christ our Lord. **Amen**.

Gospel (Matt 14:13-21)

When Jesus heard of the death of John the Baptist, he withdrew in a boat to a deserted place by himself. The crowds heard of this and followed him on foot from their towns. When he disembarked and saw the vast crowd, his heart was moved with pity for them, and he cured their sick. When it was evening, the disciples approached him and said, "This is a deserted place and it is already late; dismiss the crowds so that they can go to the villages and buy food for themselves." Jesus said to them, "There is no need for them to go away; give them some food yourselves." But they said to him, "Five loaves and two fish are all we have here." Then he said, "Bring them here to me," and he ordered the crowds to sit down on the grass. Taking the five loaves and the two fish, and looking up to heaven, he said the blessing, broke the loaves, and gave them to the disciples, who in turn gave them to the crowds. They all ate and were satisfied, and they picked up the fragments left over—twelve wicker baskets full. Those who ate were about five thousand men, not counting women and children.

Brief Silence

For Reflection

By giving what little food they have to Jesus, the disciples themselves ultimately do procure food for the crowd, just not in the way they expected. Jesus tells the disciples simply to "give them food yourselves." But the disciples cannot satisfy the crowds' hunger until they give Jesus all they have—a meager five loaves and two fish. Jesus blesses these gifts and returns them to the disciples who then have enough to feed the crowds, even with "fragments left over." It is not the meager resources we have that count, but what Jesus can do with these resources when we give all we have to him. With Jesus' power and blessing, the disciples (and we) can do what they cannot do on their own.

The real good news in this Sunday's gospel doesn't lie so much in the miracle in which the crowd's hunger is satisfied and Jesus proves his power. As wondrous as all this may be, even more wondrous still is its significance: what the disciples cannot do alone—feed the hungry crowd with meager provisions—they can do with Jesus' blessing. So can we do all things for the good of the kingdom with Jesus' blessing.

✦ Some examples of Jesus using my meager resources—"five loaves and two fish"—and making them enough for others are
. . .

Brief Silence

Prayer

Bounteous God, you satisfy us so richly with the Body and Blood of your divine Son. Bless us as we strive to follow Jesus more faithfully, nourish us on our journey, and bring us to the fullness of Life forever. We ask this through Christ our Lord. **Amen**.

Jesus calls Peter to walk to him on the stormy waters and reaches out to save him when he doubts and begins to sink. As we take time for prayer and reflection, let us open our hearts to the saving power of Jesus who is here among us . . .

Prayer

All-powerful God, even the wind and stormy seas obey Jesus' command to be still. Quiet the raging seas within us, those storms that keep us from looking only to you for protection, safety, and deliverance. We ask this through Christ our Lord. **Amen**.

Gospel (Matt 14:22-33)

After he had fed the people, Jesus made the disciples get into a boat and precede him to the other side, while he dismissed the crowds. After doing so, he went up on the mountain by himself to pray. When it was evening he was there alone. Meanwhile the boat, already a few miles offshore, was being tossed about by the waves, for the wind was against it. During the fourth watch of the night, he came toward them walking on the sea. When the disciples saw him walking on the sea they were terrified. "It is a ghost," they said, and they cried out in fear. At once Jesus spoke to them, "Take courage, it is I; do not be afraid." Peter said to him in reply, "Lord, if it is you, command me to come to you on the water." He said, "Come." Peter got out of the boat and began to walk on the water toward Jesus. But when he saw how strong the wind was he became frightened; and, beginning to sink, he cried out, "Lord, save me!" Immediately Jesus stretched out his hand and caught Peter, and said to him, "O you of little faith, why did you doubt?" After they got into the boat, the wind died down. Those who were in the boat did him homage, saying, "Truly, you are the Son of God."

Brief Silence

For Reflection

The unfolding series of events in this gospel brings into sharp
contrast divine action and human response, divine trustworthi-
ness and human doubt, divine power and human weakness. When
these contrasts clash, those who give themselves over to divine
action are saved; those who rely on their own human response
face death. This clash is evident within Peter: when he looks to
Jesus and trusts him, he walks on water; when he looks away
from Jesus to the frightening wind and waves, he begins to sink.
All Jesus' disciples must contend with this inevitable clash. We all
must choose where to look. Where we choose to look is a matter of
life or death.

In order to see Jesus (and ourselves) as the saving Presence of
God, we need the one thing Peter lacks—faith. It is only our faith
that enables us to walk on the sea of life, hear Jesus' call, and
venture out ourselves on those raging waters. We will not sink in
our faithful discipleship if we look to Jesus for our strength and
protection. In this way—looking only and constantly to Jesus—
even raging seas cannot stop us from answering Jesus' command,
"Come."

✦ I am able to keep looking to Jesus who brings Life when . . .
I cast my eyes away from Jesus when . . .

Brief Silence

Prayer

O God, you bid us always and everywhere to come to you, to trust
in your care, and to believe that you will save us. Increase our
belief and help us to look only to you on our life's journey toward
the fullness of Life you offer us. We ask this through Christ our
Lord. **Amen**.

As we celebrate Mary who has been taken body and soul into glory, let us pray and reflect on God's gracious offer that one day we too will share in God's everlasting glory . . .

Prayer

All-holy God, you bless us with every good gift. May we live our lives modeled after Mary's faithfulness and goodness, bearing Christ for others in our daily lives. We ask this through Christ our Lord. **Amen**.

Gospel (Luke 1:39-56)

Mary set out and traveled to the hill country in haste to a town of Judah, where she entered the house of Zechariah and greeted Elizabeth. When Elizabeth heard Mary's greeting, the infant leaped in her womb, and Elizabeth, filled with the Holy Spirit, cried out in a loud voice and said, "Blessed are you among women, and blessed is the fruit of your womb. And how does this happen to me, that the mother of my Lord should come to me? For at the moment the sound of your greeting reached my ears, the infant in my womb leaped for joy. Blessed are you who believed that what was spoken to you by the Lord would be fulfilled."

And Mary said: / "My soul proclaims the greatness of the Lord; / my spirit rejoices in God my Savior / for he has looked upon his lowly servant. / From this day all generations will call me blessed: / the Almighty has done great things for me, / and holy is his Name. / He has mercy on those who fear him / in every generation. / He has shown the strength of his arm, / and has scattered the proud in their conceit. / He has cast down the mighty from their thrones, / and has lifted up the lowly. / He has filled the hungry with good things, / and the rich he has sent away empty. / He has come to the help of his servant Israel /

for he has remembered his promise of mercy, / the promise he made
to our fathers, / to Abraham and his children forever."

Mary remained with her about three months and then returned
to her home.

Brief Silence

For Reflection

In the *Magnificat* Mary humbly says that "all generations will
call me blessed." Her blessedness is a reflection of her fidelity to
God's plan of salvation, her faithful yes to God's will. Because of
her own submission to God's divine plan, Elizabeth recognizes
Mary's fidelity and becomes the first of "all generations" to call
Mary blessed. Now we are the generation that calls Mary blessed.
Moreover, we too are blessed when we are faithful to God's plan
of salvation, open ourselves to God's many comings, and believe
that God is doing "great things" in and through us. In God's eyes,
those who are faithful to the divine will, those who bear God in
their own bodies for the good of others, those who name the goodness in others are the ones who will one day join Mary in receiving
God's promise of mercy and be assumed into eternal glory. Mary
has gone before us and, united with her Son in eternity, awaits our
entry into the same eschatological glory. The God who "lifted up
his lowly servant," Mary, will lift up all who, like Mary, have believed in God's word and fulfilled God's will. We all share in God's
blessedness.

✦ I am among the generations that call Mary blessed when I
. . . I am aware of my own blessedness when . . .

Brief Silence

Prayer

God of glory and blessing, you took Mary body and soul into
heaven to share in the risen Jesus' everlasting glory. May we be
open to receive your many blessings, do great things in your Son's
name, and one day share with Mary and all the saints in the fullness of glory. We ask this through Christ our Lord. **Amen**.

The Canaanite woman in this gospel persists in begging Jesus to heal her daughter. We make her prayer our own as we, too, ask Jesus to heal us and those we love . . .

Prayer

God of compassion and healing, no race or creed is excluded from your care. May we come to you with whatever burdens our hearts in confidence and persistence, knowing you grant us every good. We ask this through Christ our Lord. **Amen**.

Gospel (Matt 15:21-28)

At that time, Jesus withdrew to the region of Tyre and Sidon. And behold, a Canaanite woman of that district came and called out, "Have pity on me, Lord, Son of David! My daughter is tormented by a demon." But Jesus did not say a word in answer to her. Jesus' disciples came and asked him, "Send her away, for she keeps calling out after us." He said in reply, "I was sent only to the lost sheep of the house of Israel." But the woman came and did Jesus homage, saying, "Lord, help me." He said in reply, "It is not right to take the food of the children and throw it to the dogs." She said, "Please, Lord, for even the dogs eat the scraps that fall from the table of their masters." Then Jesus said to her in reply, "O woman, great is your faith! Let it be done for you as you wish." And the woman's daughter was healed from that hour.

Brief Silence

For Reflection

The Canaanite woman in the gospel is truly revealing her own pain in begging for Jesus' pity. What loving parent would not empathize with a child as does this gospel woman? What parent does not suffer when the child suffers? The gospel woman is clearly someone who is not self-centered, but is centered on another (her daughter). Her love trumps harshness; her hope overcomes rebuff. The woman refuses to be rebuffed even by the exclusionary and harsh words of Jesus. Nothing gets in the way of her seeking healing for her daughter "tormented by a demon." The woman "keeps calling out" to Jesus because she wants him to remove the demon—to remove the evil which separates. Her great faith moves Jesus to grant her request.

Faith, by nature, is persistent. Persistence, by nature, is single-minded. Single-mindedness, by nature, achieves the end it seeks. Like the woman in the gospel seeking healing for her daughter, our faith must be great enough to overcome barriers, must focus persistently on Jesus, and must bear the fruit of salvation and healing for others. Our faith must be strengthened by hope and spurred to action by great love.

✦ When my faith brings me to focus more persistently on Jesus, my ministry leads me to . . .

Brief Silence

Prayer

Healing God, you recognize even the weak faith of your hurting children. Help us to come to you, bearing our needs with the hope that you will draw us to yourself and ease our burdens. We ask this through Christ our Lord. **Amen**.

Jesus asks the disciples who he is, and Peter answers that he is the Christ. As we prepare for our prayer and reflection, let us open our hearts to encounter Christ and come to know him better . . .

Prayer

Wondrous God, you are beyond our knowledge, yet you reveal who your Son is to us. May we confess with our lips that Jesus is our Savior and profess by the goodness of our lives that he is risen and among us. We ask this through Christ our Lord. **Amen**.

Gospel (Matt 16:13-20)

Jesus went into the region of Caesarea Philippi and he asked his disciples, "Who do people say that the Son of Man is?" They replied, "Some say John the Baptist, others Elijah, still others Jeremiah or one of the prophets." He said to them, "But who do you say that I am?" Simon Peter said in reply, "You are the Christ, the Son of the living God." Jesus said to him in reply, "Blessed are you, Simon son of Jonah. For flesh and blood has not revealed this to you, but my heavenly Father. And so I say to you, you are Peter, and upon this rock I will build my church, and the gates of the netherworld shall not prevail against it. I will give you the keys to the kingdom of heaven. Whatever you bind on earth shall be bound in heaven; and whatever you loose on earth shall be loosed in heaven." Then he strictly ordered his disciples to tell no one that he was the Christ.

Brief Silence

For Reflection

In answer to Jesus' query about his identity, the disciples tell Jesus what *others* are saying about him. Their answer is based on hearsay. This is not good enough and does not get at the heart of who Jesus is. Jesus is not simply initiating an open discussion; he is leading the disciples to personal understanding and profession of who he is. Peter arrives there when he acclaims, "You are the Christ, the Son of the Living God." Each of us must come to this same personal profession about who Jesus is. Each of us must move beyond what others have told us about Jesus to a personal encounter with him that brings us to the awe and wonder of who he is: the Messiah who has come to save us.

Together, we are the church which is that community of individuals who have come personally to know who Jesus is and have chosen personally to make Jesus known to the world. Jesus himself will lead us there through our personal encounters with him. The building of the church begins with Peter, but continues through the ages with all those who profess who Jesus is.

✦ As I peer into the eyes of communicants, I see Jesus as . . .

Brief Silence

Prayer

Saving God, you sent your Son into our world to be our Messiah, to save us from whatever separates us from your holiness and Life. May our lives build up the church. Help us to follow Jesus faithfully and deepen our desire to know Jesus ever more personally. We ask this through Christ our Lord. **Amen**.

Jesus tells his disciples that they must lose their life in order to find it. Let us pray and reflect about what in ourselves we must lose in order to be faithful disciples of Jesus . . .

Prayer

God of the cross and resurrection, your Son embraced suffering so that we might have Life. Help us to deny ourselves for the sake of others, to come to you for the help we need to let go of our own petty desires, and to conform our lives more perfectly to Jesus' life. We ask this through Christ our Lord. **Amen**.

Gospel (Matt 16:21-27)

Jesus began to show his disciples that he must go to Jerusalem and suffer greatly from the elders, the chief priests, and the scribes, and be killed and on the third day be raised. Then Peter took Jesus aside and began to rebuke him, "God forbid, Lord! No such thing shall ever happen to you." He turned and said to Peter, "Get behind me, Satan! You are an obstacle to me. You are thinking not as God does, but as human beings do."

Then Jesus said to his disciples, "Whoever wishes to come after me must deny himself, take up his cross, and follow me. For whoever wishes to save his life will lose it, but whoever loses his life for my sake will find it. What profit would there be for one to gain the whole world and forfeit his life? Or what can one give in exchange for his life? For the Son of Man will come with his angels in his Father's glory, and then he will repay all according to his conduct."

Brief Silence

For Reflection

Jesus "began to show his disciples" what faithful discipleship demands: denying self, losing self, letting self die. The old self must give way so a new self can emerge. What we relinquish is ourselves as we are now; what we are given is a new self born from identifying completely with Jesus. It takes a lifetime of discipleship to turn from wanting to rebuke Jesus' way of living through the cross to embracing it. It takes a lifetime of discipleship to let Jesus transform our life into his Life.

Regardless of Peter's good intentions to protect his Master and Lord, Jesus turns Peter's objection to suffering and death into the profound meaning of virtually everything Jesus is about, caught in a few pithy sayings: Jesus' followers must deny themselves and take up his cross; the followers must let go of their life (self-will, human responses, human way of thinking) in order to find Life; unless one dies one cannot rise. Jesus forthrightly reveals to his disciples what awaits—death, but also resurrection. If we want to go where Jesus ultimately went—to glory—there is only one road: to Jerusalem where death awaits.

✦ Letting go of my self and receiving a new self from Jesus is evident in my life when . . .

Brief Silence

Prayer

God of glory and salvation, you are ever with us as we strive to overcome our own self-absorption and reach out to others with care and love. Transform us into being more perfect members of the Body of your Son Jesus Christ, that one day we might share in his risen glory. We ask this through Christ our Lord. **Amen**.

Jesus lays before us perhaps one of the most difficult challenges of being members of the Christian community—healing relationships which are broken. We pause now to acknowledge before God our need for healing and reconciliation . . .

Prayer

God of peace and reconciliation, you desire that your beloved children live in the peace and harmony that flow from the community of the Trinity. Help us to acknowledge our separations, beg for forgiveness and reconciliation when strife occurs, and witness to the unity you seek for us. We ask this through Christ our Lord. **Amen**.

Gospel (Matt 18:15-20)

Jesus said to his disciples: "If your brother sins against you, go and tell him his fault between you and him alone. If he listens to you, you have won over your brother. If he does not listen, take one or two others along with you, so that 'every fact may be established on the testimony of two or three witnesses.' If he refuses to listen to them, tell the church. If he refuses to listen even to the church, then treat him as you would a Gentile or a tax collector. Amen, I say to you, whatever you bind on earth shall be bound in heaven, and whatever you loose on earth shall be loosed in heaven. Again, amen, I say to you, if two of you agree on earth about anything for which they are to pray, it shall be granted to them by my heavenly Father. For where two or three are gathered together in my name, there am I in the midst of them."

Brief Silence

For Reflection

In this Sunday's gospel Jesus acknowledges inevitable conflicts arising among those living in the community of the church. Rifts in relationships between members of the church are actually rifts in the relationship with Jesus himself. This is why church conflicts cannot be ignored. Too much is at stake: our relationship with Jesus, upon which rests our relationship with each other. Not facing whatever fractures the unity of the church belies its gathering in Jesus' name. Healing fractures ensures that members of the church remain in relationship with Jesus and grow in love for one another. The impulse for resolving conflicts and preserving the unity of the church comes from Jesus himself and his continued Presence in the community. The response to Jesus must come from the members of the church and their work of reconciliation. What is essentially at stake is not merely the healing of personal rifts, but the very life of the church as a community. In this life we will never be a perfect community nor a perfect church, because we always have the human dimension at work, with its imperfections and weaknesses. Reconciliation is essential in the church because of our very identity as the Body of Christ.

✦ Eating and drinking at the table challenges me to be reconciled with another because . . .

Brief Silence

Prayer

Merciful and forgiving God, you are so patient when we are in conflict with one another. Help us to live as reconciling members of the Body of Christ, fostering the unity and love that bring us to the fullness of Life with you. We ask this through Christ our Lord. **Amen**.

We exalt the cross, the instrument of Christ's glory and our salvation. Let us pray and reflect on this great mystery of our salvation . . .

Prayer

God of salvation, your Son died on the cross so that we might have Life. Help us not to dwell on the cross as an instrument of suffering and death but to exalt the cross as the way to fullness of Life. We ask this through Christ our Lord. **Amen**.

Gospel (John 3:13-17)

Jesus said to Nicodemus: "No one has gone up to heaven except the one who has come down from heaven, the Son of Man. And just as Moses lifted up the serpent in the desert, so must the Son of Man be lifted up, so that everyone who believes in him may have eternal life."

For God so loved the world that he gave his only Son, so that he who believes in him might not perish but might have eternal life. For God did not send his Son into the world to condemn the world, but that the world might be saved through him.

Brief Silence

For Reflection

"Up" and "down" are words that capture seeming contradictions in this gospel and on this feast. The space between up and down, heaven and earth, divinity and humanity is closed by the obedience, self-emptying, and fidelity of the Son. This feast day celebrates that on the cross the Son overcomes these contradictions. We ourselves are drawn into the mystery of the cross as exaltation by our belief in the Son. Our believing bridges the space be-tween God and us, between Life and death, between being saved or perishing. However, the cost to us is the same as that for the "Son of Man": obedience, death. Yet the eternal Life that is given is worth this and any cost.

The depth of God's love for the world becomes fully revealed in the death of Jesus on the cross. The Father did not give over the Son to die, but he did give him to *us* so that we might share in his risen Life. The way to this eternal Life is through humble obedi-ence and through believing in God's "only Son." The question the gospel leaves with us is, How much do we believe?

✦ The cross, for me, is a contradiction when . . . That contra-diction is overcome when I . . .

Brief Silence

Prayer

Loving and saving God, we exalt the cross as a sign of Jesus' victory over death and being raised to eternal glory. May we live faithful to his Gospel and one day share in the promise of fullness of Life. We ask this through Christ our Lord. **Amen.**

God calls us to labor in the divine vineyard. As we prepare for our prayer and reflection, let us pause and ask God for the grace to be faithful laborers . . .

Prayer

O God, you call laborers to work in the vineyard of salvation. May our hearts always be grateful for being called to this labor of love and may we be faithful to the Gospel so that our labors are not in vain. We ask this through Christ our Lord. **Amen**.

Gospel (Matt 20:1-16a)

Jesus told his disciples this parable: "The kingdom of heaven is like a landowner who went out at dawn to hire laborers for his vineyard. After agreeing with them for the usual daily wage, he sent them into his vineyard. Going out about nine o'clock, the landowner saw others standing idle in the marketplace, and he said to them, 'You too go into my vineyard, and I will give you what is just.' So they went off. And he went out again around noon, and around three o'clock, and did likewise. Going out about five o'clock, the landowner found others standing around, and said to them, 'Why do you stand here idle all day?' They answered, 'Because no one has hired us.' He said to them, 'You too go into my vineyard.' When it was evening the owner of the vineyard said to his foreman, 'Summon the laborers and give them their pay, beginning with the last and ending with the first.' When those who had started about five o'clock came, each received the usual daily wage. So when the first came, they thought that they would receive more, but each of them also got the usual wage. And on receiving it they grumbled against the landowner, saying, 'These last ones worked only one hour, and you have made them equal to us, who bore the day's burden and the heat.' He said to one of them in reply, 'My friend, I am not cheating you. Did you not agree with me for the usual daily wage? Take what is yours and go. What if I wish to give this last one the same as you? Or am I not free to do as I wish with my own money? Are you envious because I am generous?' Thus, the last will be first, and the first will be last."

Brief Silence

For Reflection

This gospel raises the question of who is first and who is last in the kingdom of heaven. Those laborers are last who shift their focus from doing the work of the landowner to grumbling about the amount of wages others are receiving. Those are first who do not labor in the vineyard because of the amount of wages, but simply because they are privileged to share in the work of the landowner. Indeed, simply being called to the privilege of sharing in Jesus' work of salvation is its own recompense.

Simply being privileged to share in Jesus' work of salvation is already an abundant wage. The wages will take care of themselves because in this kingdom generosity overflows. To share in this superabundant generosity, we need to be willing to do the hard work of patterning our lives on Jesus' life, of giving ourselves over for the good of others, of keeping focused on the divine Landowner who calls us to labor for the sake of the kingdom. The kingdom of heaven is revealed by those who choose this work. Do we choose it? Which kind of laborer do we want to be—the first or the last?

✦ Communicants are laborers sharing in Jesus' work of salvation, and Holy Communion helps them choose to be faithful to this work in that . . .

Brief Silence

Prayer

Good God, you desire that salvation be for all people. Help us to be faithful laborers in your vineyard, learn to rely on Jesus' Presence for our fruitfulness, and one day come to share in the fullness of Life everlasting. We ask this through Christ our Lord. **Amen.**

This gospel challenges us to be honest in our response to what God asks of us and faithful in carrying out what we promise to do. Let us ask for God's mercy for the times when we have not been faithful . . .

Prayer

God of truth and mercy, you see into our hearts and know our desires. Help us always to say yes to your divine will, growing in the holiness that brings us to a share in everlasting Life with you. We ask this through Christ our Lord. **Amen**.

Gospel (Matt 21:28-32)

Jesus said to the chief priests and elders of the people: "What is your opinion? A man had two sons. He came to the first and said, 'Son, go out and work in the vineyard today.' He said in reply, 'I will not,' but afterwards changed his mind and went. The man came to the other son and gave the same order. He said in reply, 'Yes, sir,' but did not go. Which of the two did his father's will?" They answered, "The first." Jesus said to them, "Amen, I say to you, tax collectors and prostitutes are entering the kingdom of God before you. When John came to you in the way of righteousness, you did not believe him; but tax collectors and prostitutes did. Yet even when you saw that, you did not later change your minds and believe him."

Brief Silence

For Reflection

The first son's initial answer to his father was honest (he never intended to be obedient), but he "changed his mind" and did what his father asked. By contrast, the second son's seemingly obedient

"Yes, sir" in fact was dishonest—he "did not go." One changed his no to yes and did what his father asked. His changing his mind was a matter of changing his intent, his way of acting. The other changed his yes to no and revealed his true intent by not going. Yes and no are such small words that carry such huge import. The parable teaches that a firm yes to what God asks of us has much at stake: entering into the kingdom of heaven.

Jesus condemns the chief priests' and elders' behavior because of their own utter dishonesty. Challenged by the "way of righteousness" of John, the sinful tax collectors and prostitutes (like the first son) change their behavior. Trapped in their self-righteousness, the chief priests and elders (like the second son) refuse to change. Changing one's mind—choosing conversion of self—is a matter of utter honesty with self, God, and others. We are moved to conversion—to change of mind, change of heart—when we are honest enough to see within ourselves what needs to be changed.

✦ I am most open to looking honestly at myself and making necessary changes in my daily living when . . .

Brief Silence

Prayer
God of mercy and promise, you are faithful to us even when we are unfaithful to you. Help us to see ourselves honestly and embrace whatever conversion of self is necessary so that we might grow in our love for you. We ask this through Christ our Lord. **Amen**.

God desires that each of us be faithful and receive the Life the kingdom of God offers. Let us pray and reflect well so that we may grow in God's Life . . .

Prayer

Caring God, you do all you can to bring us to the vineyard of your kingdom. Help us to be faithful tenants, live the Gospel fervently, and align ourselves with the goodness of your divine Son. We ask this through Christ our Lord. **Amen.**

Gospel (Matt 21:33-43)

Jesus said to the chief priests and the elders of the people: "Hear another parable. There was a landowner who planted a vineyard, put a hedge around it, dug a wine press in it, and built a tower. Then he leased it to tenants and went on a journey. When vintage time drew near, he sent his servants to the tenants to obtain his produce. But the tenants seized the servants and one they beat, another they killed, and a third they stoned. Again he sent other servants, more numerous than the first ones, but they treated them in the same way. Finally, he sent his son to them, thinking, 'They will respect my son.' But when the tenants saw the son, they said to one another, 'This is the heir. Come, let us kill him and acquire his inheritance.' They seized him, threw him out of the vineyard, and killed him. What will the owner of the vineyard do to those tenants when he comes?" They answered him, "He will put those wretched men to a wretched death and lease his vineyard to other tenants who will give him the produce at the proper times." Jesus said to them, "Did you never read in the Scriptures: / *The stone that the builders rejected / has become the cornerstone; / by the Lord has this been done, / and it is wonderful in our eyes?* / Therefore, I say to you, the kingdom of God will be taken away from you and given to a people that will produce its fruit."

Brief Silence

For Reflection

This parable is a good example of the reality that violence tends to beget more violence. The tenants think that by being violent toward and killing the servants who come to gather the land-owner's rightful share of the produce, they will have more for themselves. This begets even more greed and violence: they think that if they kill the son, they will inherit the vineyard and have all the produce for themselves. In the end, they themselves meet with violence and have nothing—not even their own lives. The "chief priests and elders," by their own words, align themselves with the tenants in the parable—these Jewish leaders are unfaithful and ultimately they, too, kill the One God sends into the vineyard. Like the tenants, in the end they lose what they are trying to protect. They lose the inheritance of God's kingdom that has been promised to the Jewish people from of old; they will be cut off from "the kingdom of God," that is, the vine of life will be taken away from them and given to others who are faithful. Those who are faithful and accept the Son receive the Life only God's kingdom can bring. They receive the very Life of God.

✦ What it means to me to be a *tenant* (and not the owner) of God's vineyard is . . .

Brief Silence

Prayer

O God, your vineyard is a place of peace and justice, goodness and mercy. Help us to be faithful laborers in your vineyard, root out any violence that is around us, and come to inherit the Life your kingdom promises. We ask this through Christ our Lord. **Amen**.

Our heavenly King invites us to the lavish banquet of his abiding Presence. Let us prepare ourselves well for our prayer and reflection by opening ourselves to God's Presence and mercy . . .

Prayer

O God, you invite us to your heavenly banquet where we are nourished by your generous lavishness. Help us to respond to your invitation with full heart and eager willingness, and bask in your eternal Presence. We ask this through Christ our Lord. **Amen**.

Gospel (Matt 22:1-10 [Longer Form: Matt 22:1-14])

Jesus again in reply spoke to the chief priests and elders of the people in parables, saying, "The kingdom of heaven may be likened to a king who gave a wedding feast for his son. He dispatched his servants to summon the invited guests to the feast, but they refused to come. A second time he sent other servants, saying, 'Tell those invited: "Behold, I have prepared my banquet, my calves and fattened cattle are killed, and everything is ready; come to the feast."' Some ignored the invitation and went away, one to his farm, another to his business. The rest laid hold of his servants, mistreated them, and killed them. The king was enraged and sent his troops, destroyed those murderers, and burned their city. Then he said to his servants, 'The feast is ready, but those who were invited were not worthy to come. Go out, therefore, into the main roads and invite to the feast whomever you find.' The servants went out into the streets and gathered all they found, bad and good alike, and the hall was filled with guests."

Brief Silence

For Reflection

The king is adamant about filling the wedding hall with guests. His initial guest list has been carefully drawn up, but when these invited guests do not come, the king sends his servants out to invite anyone and everyone—the "bad and good alike." The hall must be filled. There can be no real feast with only a partially filled hall—the joy and happiness of the feast must be full. The bottom line issue in this parable, however, is not who is invited to fill the hall, but who will choose to come. In the same manner as the parable king, God persistently invites us to the royal banquet in the "kingdom of heaven." But the gracious invitation requires our positive and definite response.

Our response must be more than a matter of merely coming to the banquet. To share in God's banquet we must do our part. We must live our lives doing God's will. We must be faithful subjects of our divine King by being faithful disciples of the King's Son. We must choose to respond to the invitation to come to the banquet, but we must do so honestly and appropriately, with full heart and eager willingness.

✦ My daily living that witnesses to the lavishness of the eucharistic banquet summons others to God's heavenly banquet when I . . .

Brief Silence

Prayer

O God, you desire that all should share in the goodness of your heavenly banquet. May we come to the table of your Son's Body and Blood worthily and reverently, receiving from you the Life only you can give. We ask this through Christ our Lord. **Amen**.

Jesus dispels the false dichotomy between earthly kingdoms and God's kingdom. Let us reflect during our prayer on how well we have been guided by God's values and ways . . .

Prayer

O God, your kingdom is not of this world and your reign is everlasting. May we look to you as the center of our lives and choose ways for ourselves that further your reign. We ask this through Christ our Lord. **Amen**.

Gospel (Matt 22:15-21)

The Pharisees went off and plotted how they might entrap Jesus in speech. They sent their disciples to him, with the Herodians, saying, "Teacher, we know that you are a truthful man and that you teach the way of God in accordance with the truth. And you are not concerned with anyone's opinion, for you do not regard a person's status. Tell us, then, what is your opinion: Is it lawful to pay the census tax to Caesar or not?" Knowing their malice, Jesus said, "Why are you testing me, you hypocrites? Show me the coin that pays the census tax." Then they handed him the Roman coin. He said to them, "Whose image is this and whose inscription?" They replied, "Caesar's." At that he said to them, "Then repay to Caesar what belongs to Caesar and to God what belongs to God."

Brief Silence

For Reflection

Jesus is not fooled by the Pharisees' and Herodians' shameful flattery, but sees through it to their malice and hypocrisy. These vices lead to a false dichotomy between earthly and divine kingdoms.

Goodness and truth lead us to recognize our place and proper conduct in both kingdoms. When earthly kingdoms are guided by God's values and ways, they are no less than the spatial presence here and now of God's kingdom. And we pay only one tax: the self-giving that bears the image of Jesus.

When God is truly the center of our lives, and we faithfully bear the image of Jesus in all we do, our choices about responsibilities and concerns in all the various realms in which we live—family, workplace, city, nation, world, church—are clearer. Even when there is a clash of values, if we remain faithful to the image of Jesus we bear, then it is clear to others how we make our choices; how we serve; and how we tithe our time, talents, and treasure for the good of all. The fundamental choice is ours to make: to bear the image of Jesus at all times and in all places.

✦ When people look upon me and my life, the "image" and "inscription" they see is . . .

Brief Silence

Prayer

Almighty God, you created us in your divine image and imprint on us at our baptism the image of Jesus your Son. May we be faithful to this exalted identity with which you have blessed us, and live as witnesses of your risen Son's Presence among us. We ask this through Christ our Lord. **Amen**.

Jesus teaches us that everything can be summed up in loving God with our whole hearts, souls, and minds and loving our neighbor as ourselves. We ask God's pardon for our failures to love, and pray for the strength to love more generously . . .

Prayer

Gracious and faithful God, your command to love you and one another invites us into intimate relationships that bring us joy and happiness. May we be faithful to your law of love, serving you in one another. We ask this through Christ our Lord. **Amen**.

Gospel (Matt 22:34-40)

When the Pharisees heard that Jesus had silenced the Sadducees, they gathered together, and one of them, a scholar of the law, tested him by asking, "Teacher, which commandment in the law is the greatest?" He said to him, "You shall love the Lord, your God, with all your heart, with all your soul, and with all your mind. This is the greatest and the first commandment. The second is like it: You shall love your neighbor as yourself. The whole law and the prophets depend on these two commandments."

Brief Silence

For Reflection

By asking "which commandment in the law is the greatest," the Pharisees reveal an attitude toward law far different from that of Jesus. Instead of limiting the demand of the law as the Pharisees do to discrete commandments that are kept or not, Jesus teaches that the demand of the law embraces the totality of our relationships with God, self, and neighbor. We are to love God above all things and others, with our entire being. This kind of love is singular—God alone is deserving of receiving everything we are.

There is a second, similar commandment as well: we are to love our neighbor as ourselves. The love we have for our neighbor, as Jesus says, is to be the love we have for ourselves. Most of us, however, probably don't think too often about loving ourselves. This means that we care for and respect ourselves, and do the same for our neighbor. Love for self means that we don't do anything in word or action that would diminish our dignity, limit our capacity for personal growth, or dim the inner beauty of who we are. Love defines our relationships; love is the wellspring of obedience to any commandment. Love is the greatest commandment because it truly is the whole Law of God.

✦ My love of Christ in the Eucharist draws me to love the Christ found in my neighbor because . . .

Brief Silence

Prayer

Lord God, help us not to see your commandments as restrictions, but as freeing us to love as your Son loves us. May we give you our very selves in love, remain faithful to your commandments, and one day share with you the fullness of Life that is Love itself. We ask this through Christ our Lord. **Amen**.

As we honor the saints in heaven, let us pray so that we might grow in our own holiness . . .

Prayer

Holy God, you call us to the dignity and goodness that belongs to those who are faithful. May we embrace a life of blessing now and come to the fullness of Life at our journey's end. We ask this through Christ our Lord. **Amen**.

Gospel (Matt 5:1-12a)

When Jesus saw the crowds, he went up the mountain, and after he had sat down, his disciples came to him. He began to teach them, saying: / "Blessed are the poor in spirit, / for theirs is the Kingdom of heaven. / Blessed are they who mourn, / for they will be comforted. / Blessed are the meek, / for they will inherit the land. / Blessed are they who hunger and thirst for righteousness, / for they will be satisfied. / Blessed are the merciful, / for they will be shown mercy. / Blessed are the clean of heart, / for they will see God. / Blessed are the peacemakers, / for they will be called children of God. / Blessed are they who are persecuted for the sake of righteousness, / for theirs is the Kingdom of heaven. / Blessed are you when they insult you and persecute you and utter every kind of evil against you falsely because of me. Rejoice and be glad, for your reward will be great in heaven."

Brief Silence

For Reflection

The whole gamut of human emotions and needs Jesus "saw [in] the crowds" prompted him to teach his disciples the Beatitudes. Nine times Jesus uses the word "Blessed" in reference to the crowds. The prevailing notion in Jesus' time was that those who were blessed by God were wealthy, healthy, and prosperous. These were signs of God's favor. But in the Beatitudes Jesus rebuts this interpretation. Instead he calls blessed all those who would be considered unpropitious. Jesus reveals that blessedness lies in the dignity and goodness of the person as a person. No one—whether mourning or joyful, meek or bold, persecuted or at peace—is excluded from God's desire that all be blessed. The challenge of the gospel is for us to live up to this dignity and goodness, no matter what life throws our way. Blessedness is a state of living the dignity and goodness of who we are. Our condition in life now is not all there is to life. The Beatitudes, then, both show us who we are now and who we will be in the fullness of the Life to come. We are blessed, indeed!

✦ I live the dignity and goodness that is mine as one baptized into Christ Jesus when I . . .

Brief Silence

Prayer

God of blessings, you give us every good thing. Strengthen us when we face life's challenges, and help us to remember that you bless us with your very Life. We ask this through Christ our Lord. **Amen**.

As we spend time in prayer and reflection to commemorate the faithful departed, may it be our abiding hope that the souls of the just are in the hands of God. Let us join ourselves with the faithful departed . . .

Prayer

Faithful God, you desire that not one chosen by your divine Son be lost. As we remember our beloved faithful departed, help us to learn from their virtue and one day share with them in everlasting glory. We ask this through Christ our Lord. **Amen**.

Gospel (John 6:37-40 [see p. 127 for other gospel options])

Jesus said to the crowds: "Everything that the Father gives me will come to me, and I will not reject anyone who comes to me, because I came down from heaven not to do my own will but the will of the one who sent me. And this is the will of the one who sent me, that I should not lose anything of what he gave me, but that I should raise it on the last day. For this is the will of my Father, that everyone who sees the Son and believes in him may have eternal life, and I shall raise him up on the last day."

Brief Silence

For Reflection

God wills that all "have eternal life." While this gift is surely and freely given by God, it nonetheless requires something of us: belief in the Son. Rather than an intellectual consent, this belief is a consent of our self, of our will, of our life. Jesus will raise up on the "last day" those who come to him, who choose to be grasped by him, and who welcome the Life he gives. These are the faithful departed who rest in peace and whom we commemorate this day.

The gospel twice points to the hope we have for those faithful who have died but have not yet received the fullness of eternal Life: Jesus promises that "I will not reject anyone" and "I should not lose anything." The basis for this hope lies in Jesus himself who passed from death to Life. Jesus is the risen One, and the faithful departed who live their baptismal commitment join him in his risen Life. Having passed through trial and testing, the faithful departed are now graced with peace, understanding, love, and mercy. They have given their all during life, and now receive all from the Son who draws them to eternal union with him.

✦ I remember and honor my beloved dead this day by . . . They inspire me to . . .

Brief Silence

Prayer
God of hope and Life, you gave us your only-begotten Son to teach us how to live so that we might one day share fully in his risen Life. We know that we will be tested during our life and sometimes fall short of Gospel living. Help us to turn to your mercy and forgiveness. We ask this through Christ our Lord. **Amen.**

Other gospel options for November 2:
Matthew 5:1-12a / Matthew 11:25-30 / Matthew 25:31-46 / Luke 7:11-17 / Luke 23:44-46, 50, 52-53; 24:1-6a / Luke 24:13-16, 28-35 / John 5:24-29 / John 6:51-58 / John 11:17-27 / John 11:32-45 / John 14:1-6

THE DEDICATION OF THE LATERAN BASILICA

We celebrate on this Sunday the feast of the Dedication of the Lateran Basilica, which is the pope's cathedral in Rome and our mother church. As we prepare for our prayer and reflection, let us ask that we may become more perfectly who we are—the living temple of the Holy Spirit.

Prayer

O God who is ever present among us, you dwell in all of creation. Help us to live more perfectly as temples of your divine Presence and Holiness, and grow in our love for your dwelling place. May we be drawn to give your praise and glory night and day. We ask this through Christ our Lord. **Amen.**

Gospel (John 2:13-22)

Since the Passover of the Jews was near, Jesus went up to Jerusalem. He found in the temple area those who sold oxen, sheep, and doves, as well as the money changers seated there. He made a whip out of cords and drove them all out of the temple area, with the sheep and oxen, and spilled the coins of the money-changers and overturned their tables, and to those who sold doves he said, "Take these out of here, and stop making my Father's house a marketplace." His disciples recalled the words of Scripture, *Zeal for your house will consume me*. At this the Jews answered and said to him, "What sign can you show us for doing this?" Jesus answered and said to them, "Destroy this temple and in three days I will raise it up." The Jews said, "This temple has been under construction for forty-six years, and you will raise it up in three days?" But he was speaking about the temple of his Body. Therefore, when he was raised from the dead, his disciples remembered that he had said this, and they came to believe the Scripture and the word Jesus had spoken.

Brief Silence

For Reflection

"Zeal for your house will consume me." Jesus' zeal exceeds merely cleansing the temple. His zeal is for the people to be faithful to their covenant with God. His zeal did lead ultimately to the destruction of his body on the cross. But it also brought the Father on the third day to raise him to new Life. This feast of the Dedication of the Lateran Basilica in Rome is truly a feast of Life. The temple in Jerusalem was the seat of Israel's religious life, but Jesus announces an even more abundant Life—his body as temple which will be raised up after three days. Moreover, Ezekiel also envisions life—the abundant Life which flows from even a temple which is in ruins. Paul, too, speaks of life—the Life we receive in baptism whereby we ourselves become temples of the Holy Spirit and members of the Body of Christ, the church. In a sense, then, this feast is a celebration of our own life and the Life we receive from God through the church. This feast day of our mother church in Rome calls us to a zeal that will consume us when we give our lives for others as Jesus did and live the new Life given us by the Father. Are we willing to choose this zeal that consumes us?

✦ My manner of distributing Holy Communion shows zeal for love of the Body of Christ when I . . .

Brief Silence

Prayer

Zealous and jealous God, you guard us with your care and mercy. As we celebrate this festival of our cathedral church in Rome, help us to be mindful of the needs of all the church, to pray for the unity of all Christians, and to be zealous in our respect and awe for your dwelling place. We ask this through Christ our Lord. **Amen**.

To prepare for fruitful prayer, let us reflect on how faithful we have been in choosing to grow in the wealth of Life God has given us . . .

Prayer

Generous God, you have given us all we need to live a good and fruitful life. May we increase the good you have given us, produce abundant fruit for the furthering of your reign, and hear you say to us, "Well done, my good and faithful servant." We ask this through Christ our Lord. **Amen**.

Gospel (Matt 25:14-30 [Shorter Form: Matt 25:14-15, 19-21])

Jesus told his disciples this parable: "A man going on a journey called in his servants and entrusted his possessions to them. To one he gave five talents; to another, two; to a third, one—to each according to his ability. Then he went away. Immediately the one who received five talents went and traded with them, and made another five. Likewise, the one who received two made another two. But the man who received one went off and dug a hole in the ground and buried his master's money.

"After a long time the master of those servants came back and settled accounts with them. The one who had received five talents came forward bringing the additional five. He said, 'Master, you gave me five talents. See, I have made five more.' His master said to him, 'Well done, my good and faithful servant. Since you were faithful in small matters, I will give you great responsibilities. Come, share your master's joy.' Then the one who had received two talents also came forward and said, 'Master, you gave me two talents. See, I have made two more.' His master said to him, 'Well done, my good and faithful servant. Since you were faithful in small matters, I will give you great responsibilities. Come, share your master's joy.' Then the one who had received the one talent came forward and said, 'Master, I knew you were a demanding person, harvesting where you did not plant and gathering where you did not scatter; so out of fear I went off and buried your talent in the ground. Here it is back.' His master said to him in reply, 'You wicked, lazy servant! So you knew that I harvest where I did not plant and gather where I did not scatter? Should you not then have put my money in the bank so that I could have got it back with interest on my return? Now then! Take the talent from him and give it to the one with ten. For to everyone who has, more will be given and he will grow rich; but from the one who has not, even what he has will be taken away. And throw this useless servant into the darkness outside, where there will be wailing and grinding of teeth.'"

Brief Silence

For Reflection

God's Life isn't a quantity to be measured like talents. God's Life is a relationship which can never be exhausted. The curious thing about God's generosity with divine Life is that the richer in it we become, the more likely we are to be faithful in the small matters so we can grow in what we already have. No, the number of talents we have really doesn't matter in the face of God's gifts which are incalculable—ultimately, a share in the "master's joy," the messianic banquet.

Every servant in this gospel parable is given riches by the master with the expectation that each servant will increase what has been given. Even one talent was a significant amount of riches. To bury it was to waste its potential. The servant who does so out of fear, wickedness, laziness is condemned by the master upon his return and loses even what he has. The wealth each of us has been given by our Master is a share in his very Life. Even a small amount is an incalculable richness. We will be judged by how we have chosen to allow this Life to increase, to grow within us. To choose otherwise is to bury our very selves.

✦ The wealth of Life that I receive by remaining faithful to the small matters in my ministry and discipleship is . . .

Brief Silence

Prayer

Loving God, you give us the greatest gift we could ever desire: your own Life. Help us to be faithful in doing your divine will, increase our love for you, and one day bring us to the fullness of your Life. We ask this through Christ our Lord. **Amen.**

We celebrate the victory of Christ our King over death and his reign in eternal glory. Let us reflect on how well we have responded to his Presence in others and open ourselves to the kind judgment of God's mercy . . .

Prayer

God our King and Father, your rule is kind and your judgment is merciful. Help us to reach out to other persons who are in need and see in them the face of your divine Son. We ask this through Christ our Lord. **Amen**.

Gospel (Matt 25:31-46)

Jesus said to his disciples: "When the Son of Man comes in his glory, and all the angels with him, he will sit upon his glorious throne, and all the nations will be assembled before him. And he will separate them one from another, as a shepherd separates the sheep from the goats. He will place the sheep on his right and the goats on his left. Then the king will say to those on his right, 'Come, you who are blessed by my Father. Inherit the kingdom prepared for you from the foundation of the world. For I was hungry and you gave me food, I was thirsty and you gave me drink, a stranger and you welcomed me, naked and you clothed me, ill and you cared for me, in prison and you visited me.' Then the righteous will answer him and say, 'Lord, when did we see you hungry and feed you, or thirsty and give you drink? When did we see you a stranger and welcome you, or naked and clothe you? When did we see you ill or in prison, and visit you?' And the king will say to them in reply, 'Amen, I say to you, whatever you did for one of the least brothers of mine, you did for me.' Then he will say to those on his left, 'Depart from me, you accursed, into the eternal fire prepared for the devil and his angels. For I was hungry and you gave me no food, I was thirsty and you gave me no drink, a stranger and you gave me no welcome, naked and you gave me no clothing, ill and in prison, and you did not care for me.' Then they will answer and say, 'Lord, when did we see you hungry or thirsty or a stranger or naked or ill or in prison, and not minister to your needs?' He will answer them, 'Amen, I say to you, what you did not do for one of these least ones, you did not do for me.' And these will go off to eternal punishment, but the righteous to eternal life."

Brief Silence

For Reflection
"When the Son of Man comes . . . " We tend to think of Christ's final coming in judgment only in terms of the end of time. We tend to think of it as something far in the future, something we need not fear nor be too concerned about now. However, Jesus surprises us with this revelation: "When the Son of Man comes . . . " *is now in others*, no matter what their guise or condition. There is an urgency about *now*: how we respond here and now to others bears eternal consequences. How we live *now* is already a judgment upon us and already is moving us in a direction of hearing Christ the King say to us, "Come, you who are blessed" or say to us, "Depart from me." There is a propinquity—a nearness, a kinship—about *who*: the person near us is Christ and how we respond determines how we will be judged. This gospel and solemnity remind us that in Christ each person is near us, is really "kin." Each and every time we do good to another, we are doing good to Christ himself and hastening the final victory when all will be gathered in glory back to our Father in heaven.

✦ I see Christ in those coming to receive Holy Communion and I respond in my daily living by . . .

Brief Silence

THE SOLEMNITY OF OUR LORD JESUS CHRIST THE KING

Prayer

Good and gracious God, you see no one as least and everyone as worthy of your gifts and blessings. As we receive all goodness from you, help us to be generous with others, living the Gospel as your Son taught us, and look forward to that day when we share in eternal Life with you. We ask this through Christ our Lord. **Amen**.